Edgar Allan Poe *Collected Poems*

Edgar Allan Poe Collected Poems

Published by Lowe &
B. Hould Publishers®, an
imprint of Borders, Inc.
311 Maynard
Ann Arbor, MI 48104
All rights reserved.

Lowe & B. Hould
Publishers is a
registered trademark of
Borders Properties, Inc.

ISBN 0-681-07468-x
10 9 8 7 6 5 4 3 2 1

Printed and bound in
the United States of
America

Designed by Mike Savitski,
Ann Arbor, Michigan

Contents

Preface to the Poems

THESE TRIFLES are collected and republished chiefly with a view to their redemption from the many improvements to which they have been subjected while going at random "the rounds of the press." I am naturally anxious that what I have written should circulate as I wrote it, if it circulate at all. In defence of my own taste, nevertheless, it is incumbent upon me to say that I think nothing in this volume of much value to the public, or very creditable to myself. Events not to be controlled have prevented me from making, at any time, any serious effort in what, under happier circumstances, would have been the field of my choice. With me poetry has not been a purpose, but a passion; and the passion should be held in reverence; they must not—they cannot at will be excited, with an eye to the paltry compensations, or the more paltry commendations, of mankind.

E. A. P.

To —

The bowers whereat, in dreams, I see
    The wantonest singing birds,
Are lips—and all thy melody
    Of lip-begotten words—

Thine eyes, in Heaven of heart enshrined
    Then desolately fall,
O God! on my funereal mind
    Like starlight on a pall—

Thy heart—*thy* heart!—I wake and sigh,
    And sleep to dream till day
Of the truth that gold can never buy—
    Of the baubles that it may.

To —

I heed not that my earthly lot
    Hath little of earth in it—
That years of love have been forgot
    In the hatred of a minute:—
I mourn not that the desolate
    Are happier, sweet, than I,
But that *you* sorrow for *my* fate
    Who am a passer by.

To — —

Not long ago, the writer of these lines,
In the mad pride of intellectuality,
Maintained "the power of words"—denied that ever
A thought arose within the human brain
Beyond the utterance of the human tongue:
And now, as if in mockery of that boast,
Two words—two foreign soft disyllables—
Italian tones, made only to be murmured
By angels dreaming in the moonlit "dew
That hangs like chains of pearl on Hermon hill,"—
Have stirred from out the abysses of his heart,
Unthought-like thoughts that are the souls of thought,
Richer, far wilder, far diviner visions
Than even the seraph harper, Israfel
(Who has "the sweetest voice of all God's creatures"),
Could hope to utter. And I! my spells are broken.
The pen falls powerless from my shivering hand.
With thy dear name as text, though bidden by thee,
I cannot write—I cannot speak or think—
Alas! I cannot feel; for 'tis not feeling,
This standing motionless upon the golden
Threshold of the wide-open gate of dreams,
Gazing, entranced, adown the gorgeous vista,
And thrilling as I see, upon the right,
Upon the left, and all the way along,
Amid unpurpled vapors, far away
To where the prospect terminates—*thee only.*

Al Aaraaf [1]

Part I

Oh! nothing earthly save the ray
(Thrown back from flowers) of Beauty's eye,
As in those gardens where the day
Springs from the gems of Circassy—
Oh! nothing earthly save the thrill
Of melody in woodland rill;
Or (music of the passion-hearted)
Joy's voice so peacefully departed
That, like the murmur in the shell,
Its echo dwelleth and will dwell—
Oh! nothing of the dross of ours,
Yet all the beauty, all the flowers,
That list our Love, and deck our bowers—
Adorn yon world afar, afar—
The wandering star.

 'Twas a sweet time for Nesace—for there
Her world lay lolling on the golden air,
Near four bright suns—a temporary rest—
An oasis in desert of the blest.
Away—away—'mid seas of rays that roll
Empyrean splendor o'er th' unchained soul—
The soul that scarce (the billows are so dense)
Can struggle to its destin'd eminence—
To distant spheres, from time to time, she rode.
And late to ours, the favor'd one of God—

5

Collected Poems

[1] A star was discovered by Tycho Brahe, which appeared suddenly in the heavens, attained in a few days a brilliancy surpassing that of Jupiter, then as suddenly disappeared, and has never been seen since.

But, now, the ruler of an anchor'd realm,
She throws aside the sceptre—leaves the helm,
And, amid incense and high spiritual hymns,
Laves in quadruple light her angel limbs.

Now happiest, loveliest in yon lovely Earth,
Whence sprang the "Idea of Beauty" into birth
(Falling in wreaths thro' many a startled star,
Like woman's hair 'mid pearls, until, afar,
It lit on hills Achaian, and there dwelt)?
She look'd into Infinity—and knelt.
Rich clouds, for canopies, about her curled—
Fit emblems of the model of her world—
Seen but in beauty—not impeding sight
Of other beauty glittering thro' the light—
A wreath that twined each starry form around,
And all the opal'd air in color bound.

All hurriedly she knelt upon a bed
Of flowers: of lilies such as rear'd the head
[2]On the fair Capo Deucato, and sprang
So eagerly around about to hang
Upon the flying footsteps of——deep pride—
[3]Of her who lov'd a mortal—and so died.
The Sephalica, budding with young bees,
Uprear'd its purple stem around her knees.
[4]And gemmy flower, of Trebizond misnam'd—

[2]On Santa Maura—olim Deucadia.
[3]Sappho.
[4]This flower is much noticed by Lewenhoeck and Tournefort. The bee feeding upon its blossom becomes intoxicated.

Inmate of highest stars, where erst it sham'd
All other loveliness: its honied dew
(The fabled nectar that the heathen knew),
Deliriously sweet, was dropp'd from Heaven,
And fell on gardens of the unforgiven
In Trebizond—and on a sunny flower
So like its own above that, to this hour,
It still remaineth, torturing the bee
With madness, and unwonted reverie:
In Heaven, and all its environs, the leaf
And blossom of the fairy plant, in grief
Disconsolate linger—grief that hangs her head,
Repenting follies that full long have fled,
Heaving her white breast to the balmy air,
Like guilty beauty, chasten'd, and more fair:
Nyctanthes too, as sacred as the light
She fears to perfume, perfuming the night:
[5]And Clytia pondering between many a sun,
While pettish tears adown her petals run:
[6]And that aspiring flower that sprang on Earth—
And died, ere scarce exalted into birth,
Bursting its odorous heart in spirit to wing
Its way to Heaven, from garden of a king:

[5]Clytia—The Chrysanthemum Peruvianum, or, to employ a better-known term, the turnsol—which turns continually toward the sun, covers itself, like Peru, the country from which it comes, with dewy clouds which cool and refresh its flowers during the most violent heat of the day.—B. DE ST. PIERRE.
[6]There is cultivated in the king's garden at Paris, a species of serpentine aloes without prickles, whose large and beautiful flower exhales a strong odor of the vanilla, during the time of its expansion, which is very short. It does not blow till toward the month of July—you then perceive it gradually open its petals—expand them—fade and die.—ST. PIERRE.

[7]And Valisnerian lotus thither flown
From struggling with the waters of the Rhone:
[8]And thy most lovely purple perfume, Zanthe!
Isola d'oro!—Fior di Levante!

[9]And the Nelumbo bud that floats forever
With Indian Cupid down the holy river—
Fair flowers, and fairy! to whose care is given
[10]To bear the Goddess' song, in odors, up to Heaven:

"Spirit! that dwellest where,
    In the deep sky,
The terrible and fair
    In beauty vie!
Beyond the line of blue—
    The boundary of the star
Which turneth at the view
    Of thy barrier and thy bar—
Of the barrier overgone
    By the comets who were cast
From their pride and from their throne
    To be drudges till the last—
To be carriers of fire
    (The red fire of their heart)
With speed that may not tire
    And with pain that shall not part—

[7]There is found, in the Rhone, a beautiful lily of the Valisnerian kind. Its stem will stretch to the length of three or four feet, thus preserving its head above water in the swellings of the river.
[8]The Hyacinth.
[9]It is a fiction of the Indians that Cupid was first seen floating in one of these down the river Ganges, and that he loves the cradle of his childhood.
[10]And golden vials full of odors, which are the prayers of the saints.—Rev. St. John.

Who livest—that we know—
    In Eternity—we feel—
But the shadow of whose brow
    What spirit shall reveal?
Tho' the beings whom thy Nesace,
    Thy messenger hath known
Have dream'd for thy Infinity
[11]A model of their own—
Thy will is done, oh, God!
    The star hath ridden high
Thro' many a tempest, but she rode
    Beneath thy burning eye;
And here, in thought, to thee—
    In thought that can alone
Ascend thy empire, and so be
    A partner of thy throne—

[11]The Humanitarians held that God was to be understood as having really a human form.—VIDE CLARKE'S SERMON, vol. i., page 26, fol. edit.

The drift of Milton's argument leads him to employ language which would appear, at first sight, to verge upon their doctrine; but it will be seen immediately that he guards himself against the charge of having adopted one of the most ignorant errors of the dark ages of the church.—DR. SUMNER'S NOTES ON MILTON'S CHRISTIAN DOCTRINE.

This opinion, in spite of many testimonies to the contrary, could never have been very general. Andeus, a Syrian of Mesopotamia, was condemned for the opinion as heretical. He lived in the beginning of the fourth century. His disciples were called Anthropmorphites.—VIDE DU PIN.

Among Milton's minor poems are these lines:

> Dicite sacrorum præsides nemorum Deæ &c.
> Quis ille primus cujus ex imagine
> Natura solers finxit humanum genus?
> Eternus, incorruptus, æquævus polo,
> Unusque et universus exemplar Dei.

And afterward:

> Non cui profundum Cæcitas lumen dedit
> Dircæus augur vidit hunc alto sinu, &c.

¹²By winged Fantasy,
   My embassy is given,
Till secrecy shall knowledge be
   In the environs of Heaven."

She ceas'd—and buried then her burning cheek
Abash'd, amid the lilies there, to seek
A shelter from the fervor of His eye;
For the stars trembled at the Deity.
She stirr'd not—breath'd not—for a voice was there
How solemnly pervading the calm air!
A sound of silence on the startled ear
Which dreamy poets name "the music of the sphere."
Ours is a world of words: Quiet we call
"Silence"—which is the merest word of all.
All Nature speaks, and ev'n ideal things
Flap shadowy sounds from visionary wings—
But ah! not so when, thus, in realms on high
The eternal voice of God is passing by,
And the red winds are withering in the sky!
¹³"What tho' in worlds which sightless cycles run,
Link'd to a little system, and one sun—
Where all my love is folly and the crowd
Still think my terrors but the thunder cloud,
The storm, the earthquake, and the ocean-wrath—
(Ah! will they cross me in my angrier path?)
What tho' in worlds which own a single sun

¹² Seltsumen Tochter Jovis
   Seinem Schosskinde
     Der Phantasie.—GOETHE.
¹³Sightless—too small to be seen.—LEGGE.

The sands of Time grow dimmer as they run,
Yet thine is my resplendency, so given
To bear my secrets thro' the upper Heaven.
Leave tenantless thy crystal home, and fly,
With all thy train, athwart the moony sky—
[14]Apart—like fire-flies in Sicilian night,
And wing to other worlds another light!
Divulge the secrets of thy embassy
To the proud orbs that twinkle—and so be
To ev'ry heart a barrier and a ban
Lest the stars totter in the guilt of man!"

Up rose the maiden in the yellow night,
The single-mooned eve!—on Earth we plight
Our faith to one love—and one moon adore—
The birth-place of young Beauty had no more.
As sprang that yellow star from downy hours
Up rose the maiden from her shrine of flowers,
And bent o'er sheeny mountain and dim plain
[15]Her way—but left not yet her Therasæan reign.

Part II

High on a mountain of enamell'd head—
Such as the drowsy shepherd on his bed
Of giant pasturage lying at his ease,
Raising his heavy eyelid, starts and sees

---

[14]I have often noticed a peculiar movement of the fire-flies;—they will collect in a body and fly off, from a common centre, into innumerable radii.

[15]Therasæa, or Therasea, the island mentioned by Seneca, which, in a moment, arose from the sea to the eyes of astonished mariners.

With many a mutter'd "hope to be forgiven"
What time the moon is quadrated in Heaven —
Of rosy head, that towering far away
Into the sunlit ether, caught the ray
Of sunken suns at eve—at noon of night,
While the moon danc'd with the fair stranger light—
Uprear'd upon such height arose a pile
Of gorgeous columns on th' unburthen'd air,
Flashing from Parian marble that twin smile
Far down upon the wave that sparkled there,
And nursled the young mountain in its lair.
[16]Of molten stars their pavement, such as fall
Thro' the ebon air, besilvering the pall
Of their own dissolution, while they die—
Adorning then the dwellings of the sky.
A dome, by linked light from Heaven let down,
Sat gently on these columns as a crown—
A window of one circular diamond, there,
Look'd out above into the purple air,
And rays from God shot down that meteor chain
And hallow'd all the beauty twice again,
Save when, between th' Empyrean and that ring,
Some eager spirit flapp'd his dusky wing.
But on the pillars Seraph eyes have seen
The dimness of this world; that greyish green
That Nature loves the best for Beauty's grave
Lurk'd in each cornice, round each architrave—

[16]Some star which, from the ruin'd roof
Of shak'd Olympus, by mischance, did fall.—MILTON.

And every sculptur'd cherub thereabout,
That from his marble dwelling peered out,
Seem'd earthly in the shadow of his niche—
Achaian statues in a world so rich!
[17]Friezes from Tadmor and Persepolis
From Balbec, and the stilly, clear abyss
[18]Of beautiful Gomorrah! Oh! the wave
Is now upon thee—but too late to save!

Sound loves to revel in a summer night:
Witness the murmur of the grey twilight
[19]That stole upon the ear, in Eyraco,
Of many a wild star-gazer long ago—
That stealeth ever on the ear of him
Who, musing, gazeth on the distance dim,
And sees the darkness coming as a cloud—
[20]Is not its form—its voice—most palpable and loud?
But what is this?—it cometh—and it brings
A music with it—'tis the rush of wings—
A pause—and then a sweeping, falling strain,
And Nesace is in her halls again.

---

[17]Voltaire, in speaking of Persepolis, says: "Je connois bien l'admiration qu'inspirent ces ruines—mais un palais érigé au pied d'une chaine des rochers sterils—peut il être un chef-d'œuvre des arts?"

[18]"Oh! the wave!"—Ula Deguisi is the Turkish appellation; but, on its own shores, it is called Bahar Loth, or Almotanah. There were undoubtedly more than two cities engulfed in the "dead sea." In the valley of Siddim were five—Adrah, Zeboin, Zoar, Sodom, and Gomorrah. Stephen of Byzantium mentions eight, and Strabo thirteen (engulfed),—but the last is out of all reason.

It is said [Tacitus, Strabo, Josephus, Daniel of St. Saba, Nau, Mundrell, Troilo, D'Arvieux], that after an excessive drought, the vestiges of columns, walls, etc., are seen above the surface. At *any* season, such remains may be discovered by looking down into the transparent lake, and at such distances as would argue the existence of many settlements in the space now usurped by the "Asphalties."

[19]Eyraco—Chaldea.

[20]I have often thought I could distinctly hear the sound of the darkness as it stole over the horizon.

From the wild energy of wanton haste
　　Her cheeks were flushing, and her lips apart;
And zone that clung around her gentle waist
　　Had burst beneath the heaving of her heart.
Within the centre of that hall to breathe
She paus'd and panted, Zanthe! all beneath,
The fairy light that kiss'd her golden hair
And long'd to rest, yet could but sparkle there!

　　[21]Young flowers were whispering in melody
To happy flowers that night—and tree to tree;
Fountains were gushing music as they fell
In many a star-lit grove, or moon-lit dell;
Yet silence came upon material things—
Fair flowers, bright waterfalls and angel wings—
And sound alone that from the spirit sprang
Bore burthen to the charm the maiden sang:

" 'Neath blue-bell or streamer—
　　Or tufted wild spray
That keeps, from the dreamer,
[22]The moonbeam away—
Bright beings! that ponder,
　　With half-closing eyes,
On the stars, which your wonder
　　Hath drawn from the skies,
Till they glance thro' the shade, and

---

[21]Fairies use flowers for their charactery.—MERRY WIVES OF WINDSOR.
[22]In Scripture is this passage—"The sun shall not harm thee by day, nor the moon by night." It is perhaps not generally known that the moon, in Egypt, has the effect of producing blindness to those who sleep with the face exposed to its rays, to which circumstance the passage evidently alludes.

Come down to your brow
Like —— eyes of the maiden
    Who calls on you now—
Arise! from your dreaming
    In violet bowers,
To duty beseeming
    These star-litten hours—
And shake from your tresses
    Encumber'd with dew
The breath of those kisses
    That cumber them too—
(Oh, how, without you, Love!
    Could angels be blest?)
Those kisses of true love
    That lull'd ye to rest!
Up!—shake from your wing
    Each hindering thing:
The dew of the night—
    It would weigh down your flight
And true love caresses—
    Oh! leave them apart!
    They are light on the tresses,
        But lead on the heart.

    "Ligeia! Ligeia!
    My beautiful one!
Whose harshest idea
    Will to melody run,
Oh! is it thy will
    On the breezes to toss?

Or, capriciously still,
[23]Like the lone Albatross,
Incumbent on night
    (As she on the air)
To keep watch with delight
    On the harmony there?

    "Ligeia! wherever
    Thy image may be,
No magic shall sever
    Thy music from thee.
Thou hast bound many eyes
    In a dreamy sleep—
    But the strains still arise
    Which *thy* vigilance keep—
The sound of the rain
    Which leaps down to the flower,
And dances again
    In the rhythm of the shower—
[24]The murmur that springs
    From the growing of grass
    Are the music of things—
    But are modell'd, alas!—
Away, then, my dearest,
    Oh! hie thee away
To springs that lie clearest
    Beneath the moon-ray—

---

[23]The albatross is said to sleep on the wing.
[24]I met with this idea in an old English tale, which I am now unable to obtain, and quote from memory.—
"The verie essence and, as it were, springe-heade and origine of all musiche is the verie pleasaunte sounde which the trees of the forest do make when they growe."

To lone lake that smiles,
   In its dream of deep rest,
At the many star-isles
   That enjewel its breast—
Where wild flowers, creeping,
   Have mingled their shade,
On its margin is sleeping
   Full many a maid—
Some have left the cool glade, and
   [25]Have slept with the bee—
Arouse them, my maiden,
   On moorland and lea—
Go! breathe on their slumber,
   All softly in ear,
The musical number
   They slumber'd to hear—
For what can awaken
   An angel so soon
Whose sleep hath been taken
   Beneath the cold moon,
As the spell which no slumber
   Of witchery may test,
The rhythmical number
   Which lull'd him to rest?"

---

[25]The wild bee will not sleep in the shade if there be moonlight.
The rhyme in this verse, as in one about sixty lines before, has an appearance of affectation. It is, however, imitated from Sir W. Scott, or rather from Claud Halcro—in whose mouth I admired its effect:

     Oh! were there an island,
       Tho' ever so wild
     Where woman might smile, and
       No man be beguil'd, etc.

Spirits in wing, and angels to the view,
A thousand seraphs burst th' Empyrean thro',
Young dreams still hovering on their drowsy flight—
Seraphs in all but "Knowledge," the keen light
That fell, refracted, thro' thy bounds, afar,
O Death! from eye of God upon that star:
Sweet was that error—sweeter still that death—
Sweet was that error—ev'n with *us* the breath
Of Science dims the mirror of our joy—
To them 'twere the Simoom; and would destroy—
For what (to them) availeth it to know
That Truth is Falsehood—or that Bliss is Woe?
Sweet was their death—with them to die was rife
With the last ecstasy of satiate life—
Beyond that death no immortality—
But sleep that pondereth is not "to be"—
And there—oh! may my weary spirit dwell—
[26]Apart from Heaven's Eternity—and yet how far from
    Hell!
What guilty spirit, in what shrubbery dim,

---

[26]With the Arabians there is a medium between Heaven and Hell, where men suffer no punishment, but yet do not attain that tranquil and even happiness which they suppose to be characteristic of heavenly enjoyment.

> Un no rompido sueno—
> Un dia puro—allegre—libre
> Quiera—
> Libre de amor—de zelo—
> De odio—de esperanza—de rezelo.—LUIS PONCE DE LEON.

Sorrow is not excluded from "Al Aaraaf," but it is that sorrow which the living love to cherish for the dead, and which, in some minds, resembles the delirium of opium. The passionate excitement of Love and the buoyancy of spirit attendant upon intoxication are its less holy pleasures—the price of which, to those souls who make choice of "Al Aaraaf" as their residence after life, is final death and annihilation.

Heard not the stirring summons of that hymn?
But two: they fell: for Heaven no grace imparts
To those who hear not for their beating hearts.
A maiden-angel and her seraph-lover—
Oh! where (and ye may seek the wide skies over)
Was Love, the blind, near sober Duty known?
[27]Unguided Love hath fallen—'mid "tears of perfect moan."

He was a goodly spirit—he who fell:
A wanderer by mossy-mantled well—
A gazer on the lights that shine above—
A dreamer in the moonbeam by his love:
What wonder? for each star is eye-like there,

And looks so sweetly down on Beauty's hair—
And they, and ev'ry mossy spring were holy
To his love-haunted heart and melancholy.
The night had found (to him a night of woe)
Upon a mountain crag, young Angelo—
Beetling it bends athwart the solemn sky,
And scowls on starry worlds that down beneath it lie.
Here sat he with his love—his dark eye bent
With eagle gaze along the firmament:
Now turn'd it upon her—but ever then
It trembled to the orb of EARTH again.
"Ianthe, dearest, see! how dim that ray!
How lovely 'tis to look so far away!
She seem'd not thus upon that autumn eve

There be tears of perfect moan
Wept for thee in Helicon.—MILTON.

I left her gorgeous halls—nor mourn'd to leave.
That eve—that eve—I should remember well—
The sun-ray dropp'd, in Lemnos, with a spell
On th' Arabesque carving of a gilded hall
Wherein I sat, and on the draperied wall—
And on my eyelids—O the heavy light!
How drowsily it weigh'd them into night!
On flowers, before, and mist, and love they ran
With Persian Saadi in his Gulistan:
But O that light!—I slumber'd—Death, the while,
Stole o'er my senses in that lovely isle
So softly that no single silken hair
Awoke that slept—or knew that he was there.

"The last spot of Earth's orb I trod upon
[28]Was a proud temple call'd the Parthenon—
More beauty clung around her column'd wall
[29]Than ev'n thy glowing bosom beats withal;
And when old Time my wing did disenthral
Thence sprang I—as the eagle from his tower,
And years I left behind me in an hour.
What time upon her airy bounds I hung
One half the garden of her globe was flung,
Unrolling as a chart unto my view—
Tenantless cities of the desert too!
Ianthe, beauty crowded on me then,
And half I wish'd to be again of men."

[28]It was entire in 1687—the most elevated spot in Athens.
[29]Shadowing more beauty in their airy brows
Than have the white breasts of the Queen of Love.—MARLOWE.

"My Angelo! and why of them to be?
A brighter dwelling-place is here for thee—
And greener fields than in yon world above,
And woman's loveliness—and passionate love."

"But, list, Ianthe! when the air so soft
[30]Fail'd, as my pennon'd spirit leapt aloft,
Perhaps my brain grew dizzy—but the world
I left so late was into chaos hurl'd—
Sprang from her station, on the winds apart,
And roll'd, a flame, the fiery Heaven athwart.
Methought, my sweet one, then I ceased to soar
And fell—not swiftly as I rose before,
But with a downward, tremulous motion thro'
Light, brazen rays, this golden star unto!
Nor long the measure of my falling hours,
For nearest of all stars was thine to ours—
Dread star! that came, amid a night of mirth,
A red Dædalion on the timid Earth.

"We came—and to thy Earth—but not to us
Be given our lady's bidding to discuss:
We came, my love; around, above, below,
Gay fire-fly of the night we come and go,
Nor ask a reason save the angel-nod
She grants to us, as granted by her God—
But, Angelo, than thine gray Time unfurl'd
Never his fairy wing o'er fairer world!
Dim was its little disk, and angel eyes

---

[30]Pennon—for opinion.—MILTON.

Alone could see the phantom in the skies,
When first Al Aaraaf knew her course to be
Headlong thitherward o'er the starry sea—
But when its glory swell'd upon the sky,
As glowing Beauty's bust beneath man's eye,
We paus'd before the heritage of men,
And thy star trembled—as doth Beauty then!"

Thus, in discourse, the lovers whiled away
The night that waned and waned and brought no day.
They fell: for Heaven to them no hope imparts
Who hear not for the beating of their hearts.

Alone

From childhood's hour I have not been
As others were—I have not seen
As others saw—I could not bring
My passions from a common spring.
From the same source I have not taken
My sorrow; I could not awaken
My heart to joy at the same tone;
And all I lov'd, *I* lov'd alone.
Then—in my childhood—in the dawn
Of a most stormy life—was drawn
From ev'ry depth of good and ill
The mystery which binds me still:
From the torrent, or the fountain,
From the red cliff of the mountain,
From the sun that 'round me roll'd
In its autumn tint of gold—
From the lightning in the sky
As it pass'd me flying by—
From the thunder and the storm,
And the cloud that took the form
(When the rest of Heaven was blue)
Of a demon in my view.

Annabel Lee

It was many and many a year ago,
    In a kingdom by the sea,
That a maiden there lived whom you may know
    By the name of ANNABEL LEE;
And this maiden she lived with no other thought
    Than to love and be loved by me.

I was a child and *she* was a child,
    In this kingdom by the sea:
But we loved with a love that was more than love—
    I and my ANNABEL LEE;
With a love that the winged seraphs of heaven
    Coveted her and me.

And this was the reason that, long ago,
    In this kingdom by the sea,
A wind blew out of a cloud, chilling
    My beautiful ANNABEL LEE;
So that her high-born kinsman came
    And bore her away from me,
To shut her up in a sepulchre
    In this kingdom by the sea.

The angels, not half so happy in heaven,
    Went envying her and me—
Yes!—that was the reason (as all men know,
    In this kingdom by the sea)
That the wind came out of the cloud by night,
    Chilling and killing my ANNABEL LEE.

But our love it was stronger by far than the love
   Of those who were older than we—
   Of many far wiser than we—
And neither the angels in heaven above,
   Nor the demons down under the sea,
Can ever dissever my soul from the soul
   Of the beautiful ANNABEL LEE,

For the moon never beams, without bringing me dreams
   Of the beautiful ANNABEL LEE;
And the stars never rise, but I feel the bright eyes
   Of the beautiful ANNABEL LEE;
And so, all the night-tide, I lie down by the side
Of my darling—my darling—my life and my bride,
   In the sepulchre there by the sea,
   In her tomb by the sounding sea.

For Annie

Thank Heaven! the crisis—
    The danger is past,
And the lingering illness
    Is over at last—
And the fever called "Living"
    Is conquered at last.
Sadly I know
    I am shorn of my strength,
And no muscle I move
    As I lie at full length—
But no matter!—I feel
    I am better at length.

And I rest so composed,
    Now, in my bed,
That any beholder
    Might fancy me dead—
Might start at beholding me,
    Thinking me dead.
The moaning and groaning,
    The sighing and sobbing,
Are quieted now,
    With that horrible throbbing
At heart:—ah, that horrible,
    Horrible throbbing!
The sickness—the nausea—
    The pitiless pain—
Have ceased, with the fever
    That maddened my brain—

With the fever called "Living"
    That burned in my brain.

And oh! of all tortures
    That torture the worst
Has abated—the terrible
    Torture of thirst
For the naphthaline river
    Of Passion accurst:—
I have drunk of a water
    That quenches all thirst:—

Of a water that flows,
    With a lullaby sound,
From a spring but a very few
    Feet under ground—
From a cavern not very far
    Down under ground.

And ah! let it never
    Be foolishly said
That my room it is gloomy
    And narrow my bed;
For man never slept
    In a different bed—
And, to *sleep,* you must slumber
    In just such a bed.

My tantalized spirit
    Here blandly reposes,
Forgetting, or never
    Regretting, its roses—

Its old agitations
  Of myrtles and roses:

For now, while so quietly
  Lying, it fancies
A holier odor
  About it, of pansies—
A rosemary odor,
  Commingled with pansies—
With rue and the beautiful
  Puritan pansies.

And so it lies happily,
  Bathing in many
A dream of the truth
  And the beauty of Annie—
Drowned in a bath
  Of the tresses of Annie.

She tenderly kissed me,
  She fondly caressed,
And then I fell gently
  To sleep on her breast—
Deeply to sleep
  From the heaven of her breast.

When the light was extinguished
  She covered me warm,
And she prayed to the angels
  To keep me from harm—
To the queen of the angels
  To shield me from harm.

And I lie so composedly,
    Now in my bed,
(Knowing her love,)
    That you fancy me dead—
And I rest so contentedly,
    Now in my bed,
(With her love at my breast,)
    That you fancy me dead—
That you shudder to look at me,
    Thinking me dead:—

But my heart is brighter
    Than all of the many
Stars in the sky,
    For it sparkles with Annie—
It glows with the light
    Of the love of my Annie—
With the thought of the light
    Of the eyes of my Annie.

The Bells

I

Hear the sledges with the bells—
Silver bells!
What a world of merriment their melody foretells!
How they tinkle, tinkle, tinkle,
In the icy air of night!
While the stars that oversprinkle
All the heavens seem to twinkle
With a crystalline delight;
Keeping time, time, time,
In a sort of Runic rhyme,
To the tintinnabulation that so musically wells
From the bells, bells, bells, bells,
Bells, bells, bells—
From the jingling and the tinkling of the bells.

II

Hear the mellow wedding bells,
Golden bells!
What a world of happiness their harmony foretells!
Through the balmy air of night
How they ring out their delight!
From the molten-golden notes,
And all in tune,
What a liquid ditty floats
To the turtle-dove that listens, while she gloats
On the moon!
Oh, from out the sounding cells
What a gush of euphony voluminously wells!

How it swells!
How it dwells
On the Future! how it tells
Of the rapture that impels
To the swinging and the ringing
Of the bells, bells, bells,
Of the bells, bells, bells, bells,
Bells, bells, bells—
To the rhyming and the chiming of the bells!

III

Hear the loud alarum bells—
Brazen bells!
What a tale of terror, now, their turbulency tells!
In the startled ear of night
How they scream out their affright!
Too much horrified to speak,
They can only shriek, shriek,
Out of tune,
In a clamorous appealing to the mercy of the fire,
In a mad expostulation with the deaf and frantic fire,
Leaping higher, higher, higher,
With a desperate desire,
And a resolute endeavor
Now—now to sit, or never,
By the side of the pale-faced moon.
Oh, the bells, bells, bells!
What a tale their terror tells
Of despair!

How they clang, and clash, and roar!
What a horror they outpour
On the bosom of the palpitating air!
Yet the ear it fully knows,
By the twanging,
And the clanging,
How the danger ebbs and flows;
Yet the ear distinctly tells,
In the jangling,
And the wrangling,
How the danger sinks and swells,
By the sinking or the swelling in the anger of the bells—
Of the bells—
Of the bells, bells, bells, bells,
Bells, bells, bells—
In the clamor and the clangor of the bells!

IV

Hear the tolling of the bells—
Iron bells!
What a world of solemn thought their melody compels!
In the silence of the night,
How we shiver with affright
At the melancholy menace of their tone!
For every sound that floats
From the rust within their throats
Is a groan.
And the people—ah, the people—
They that dwell up in the steeple,

All alone,
And who tolling, tolling, tolling,
In that muffled monotone,
Feel a glory in so rolling
On the human heart a stone—
They are neither man nor woman—
They are neither brute nor human—
They are Ghouls:
And their king it is who tolls;
And he rolls, rolls, rolls,
Rolls
A pæan from the bells!
And his merry bosom swells
With the pæan of the bells!
And he dances, and he yells;
Keeping time, time, time,
In a sort of Runic rhyme,
To the pæan of the bells—
Of the bells:
Keeping time, time, time,
In a sort of Runic rhyme,
To the throbbing of the bells—
Of the bells, bells, bells—
To the sobbing of the bells;
Keeping time, time, time,
As he knells, knells, knells,
In a happy Runic rhyme,
To the rolling of the bells—

Of the bells, bells, bells—
To the tolling of the bells,
Of the bells, bells, bells, bells—
Bells, bells, bells—
To the moaning and the groaning of the bells.

Bridal Ballad

The ring is on my hand,
    And the wreath is on my brow;
Satins and jewels grand
Are all at my command,
    And I am happy now.

And my lord he loves me well;
    But when first he breathed his vow
I felt my bosom swell—
For the words rang as a knell,
And the voice seemed *his* who fell
In the battle down the dell,
    And who is happy now.

But he spoke to reassure me,
And he kissed my pallid brow,
While a revery came o'er me,
And to the church-yard bore me,
And I sighed to him before me,
Thinking him dead D'Elormie,
    "Oh, I am happy now!"

And thus the words were spoken,
    And this the plighted vow,
And though my faith be broken,
And though my heart be broken,
Behold the golden token
    That *proves* me happy now!

Would God I could awaken!
   For I dream I know not how,
And my soul is sorely shaken
Lest an evil step be taken,—
Lest the dead who is forsaken
   May not be happy now.

The City in the Sea

Lo! Death has reared himself a throne
In a strange city lying alone
Far down within the dim West
Where the good and the bad and the worst and the best
Have gone to their eternal rest.
There shrines and palaces and towers
(Time-eaten towers that tremble not!)
Resemble nothing that is ours.
Around, by lifting winds forgot,
Resignedly beneath the sky
The melancholy waters lie.

No rays from the holy Heaven come down
On the long night-time of that town;
But light from out the lurid sea
Streams up the turrets silently—
Gleams up the pinnacles far and free—
Up domes—up spires—up kingly halls—
Up fanes—up Babylon-like walls—
Up shadowy long-forgotten bowers
Of sculptured ivy and stone flowers—
Up many and many a marvellous shrine
Whose wreathed friezes intertwine
The viol, the violet, and the vine.
Resignedly beneath the sky
The melancholy waters lie.
So blend the turrets and shadows there
That all seem pendulous in air,
While from a proud tower in the town
Death looks gigantically down.

There open fanes and gaping graves
Yawn level with the luminous waves;
But not the riches there that lie
In each idol's diamond eye—
Not the gayly-jewelled dead
Tempt the waters from their bed;
For no ripples curl, alas!
Along that wilderness of glass—
No swellings tell that winds may be
Upon some far-off happier sea—
No heavings hint that winds have been
On seas less hideously serene.

But lo, a stir is in the air!
The wave—there is a movement there!
As if the towers had thrust aside,
In slightly sinking, the dull tide—
As if their tops had feebly given
A void within the filmy Heaven.
The waves have now a redder glow—
The hours are breathing faint and low—
And when, amid no earthly moans,
Down, down that town shall settle hence,
Hell, rising from a thousand thrones,
Shall do it reverence.

The Coliseum

Type of the antique Rome! Rich reliquary
Of lofty contemplation left to Time
By buried centuries of pomp and power!
At length—at length—after so many days
Of weary pilgrimage and burning thirst
(Thirst for the springs of lore that in thee lie),
I kneel, an altered and an humble man,
Amid thy shadows, and so drink within
My very soul thy grandeur, gloom, and glory!

Vastness! and Age! and Memories of Eld!
Silence! and Desolation! and dim Night!
I feel ye now—I feel ye in your strength—
O spells more sure than e'er Judæan king
Taught in the gardens of Gethsemane!
O charms more potent than the rapt Chaldee
Ever drew down from out the quiet stars!

Here, where a hero fell, a column falls!
Here, where a mimic eagle glared in gold,
A midnight vigil holds the swarthy bat!
Here, where the dames of Rome their gilded hair
Waved to the wind, now wave the reed and thistle!
Here, where on golden throne the monarch lolled,
Glides, spectre-like, unto his marble home,
Lit by the wan light of the hornèd moon,
The swift and silent lizard of the stones!

But stay! these walls—these ivy-clad arcades—
These mouldering plinths—these sad and blackened shafts—
These vague entablatures—this crumbling frieze—

These shattered cornices—this wreck—this ruin—
These stones—alas! these gray stones—are they all—
All of the famed, and the colossal left
By the corrosive Hours to Fate and me?

"Not all"—the Echoes answer me—"not all!
Prophetic sounds and loud arise forever
From us, and from all Ruin, unto the wise,
As melody from Memnon to the Sun.
We rule the hearts of mightiest men—we rule
With a despotic sway all giant minds.
We are not impotent—we pallid stones.
Not all our power is gone—not all our fame—
Not all the magic of our high renown—
Not all the wonder that encircles us—
Not all the mysteries that in us lie—
Not all the memories that hang upon
And cling around about us as a garment,
Clothing us in a robe of more than glory."

The Conqueror Worm

Lo! 'tis a gala night
   Within the lonesome latter years!
An angel throng, bewinged, bedight
   In veils, and drowned in tears,
Sit in a theatre, to see
   A play of hopes and fears,
While the orchestra breathes fitfully
   The music of the spheres.

Mimes, in the form of God on high,
   Mutter and mumble low,
And hither and thither fly—
   Mere puppets they, who come and go
At bidding of vast formless things
   That shift the scenery to and fro,
Flapping from out their Condor wings
   Invisible Woe!

That motley drama—oh, be sure
   It shall not be forgot!
With its Phantom chased for evermore,
   By a crowd that seize it not,
Through a circle that ever returneth in
   To the self-same spot,
And much of Madness, and more of Sin,
   And Horror the soul of the plot.

But see, amid the mimic rout
   A crawling shape intrude!
A blood-red thing that writhes from out
   The scenic solitude!

It writhes!—it writhes!—with mortal pangs
    The mimes become its food,
And the angels sob at vermin fangs
    In human gore imbued.

Out—out are the lights—out all!
    And, over each quivering form,
The curtain, a funeral pall,
    Comes down with the rush of a storm,
And the angels, all pallid and wan,
    Uprising, unveiling, affirm
That the play is the tragedy "Man,"
    And its hero the Conqueror Worm.

A Dream

In visions of the dark night
   I have dreamed of joy departed;
But a waking dream of life and light
   Hath left me broken-hearted.

Ah! what is not a dream by day
   To him whose eyes are cast
On things around him, with a ray
   Turned back upon the past?

That holy dream, that holy dream,
   While all the world were chiding,
Hath cheered me as a lovely beam
   A lonely spirit guiding.

What though that light, thro' storm and night,
   So trembled from afar—
What could there be more purely bright
   In Truth's day-star?

A Dream Within a Dream

Take this kiss upon the brow!
And, in parting from you now,
Thus much let me avow—
You are not wrong, who deem
That my days have been a dream;
Yet if hope has flown away
In a night, or in a day,
In a vision, or in none,
Is it therefore the less *gone?*
All that we see or seem
Is but a dream within a dream.

I stand amid the roar
Of a surf-tormented shore,
And I hold within my hand
Grains of the golden sand—
How few! yet how they creep
Through my fingers to the deep,
While I weep—while I weep!
O God! can I not grasp
Them with a tighter clasp?
O God! can I not save
One from the pitiless wave?
Is *all* that we see or seem
But a dream within a dream?

Dream-Land

By a route obscure and lonely,
Haunted by ill angels only,
Where an Eidolon, named NIGHT,
On a black throne reigns upright,
I have reached these lands but newly
From an ultimate dim Thule—
From a wild weird clime that lieth, sublime,
      Out of SPACE—out of TIME.

Bottomless vales and boundless floods,
And chasms, and caves, and Titan woods,
With forms that no man can discover
For the dews that drip all over;
Mountains toppling evermore
Into seas without a shore;
Seas that restlessly aspire,
Surging, unto skies of fire;
Lakes that endlessly outspread
Their lone waters—lone and dead,—
Their still waters—still and chilly
With the snows of the lolling lily.

By the lakes that thus outspread
Their lone waters, lone and dead,—
Their sad waters, sad and chilly
With the snows of the lolling lily,—
By the mountains—near the river
Murmuring lowly, murmuring ever,—
By the gray woods,—by the swamp
Where the toad and the newt encamp,—
By the dismal tarns and pools

Where dwell the Ghouls,—
By each spot the most unholy—
In each nook most melancholy,—
There the traveller meets aghast
Sheeted Memories of the Past—
Shrouded forms that start and sigh
As they pass the wanderer by—
White-robed forms of friends long given,
In agony, to the Earth—and Heaven.

For the heart whose woes are legion
'Tis a peaceful, soothing region—
For the spirit that walks in shadow
'Tis—oh, 'tis an Eldorado!
But the traveller, travelling through it,
May not—dare not openly view it;
Never its mysteries are exposed
To the weak human eye unclosed;
So wills its King, who hath forbid
The uplifting of the fringed lid;
And thus the sad Soul that here passes
Beholds it but through darkened glasses.

By a route obscure and lonely,
Haunted by ill angels only,
Where an Eidolon, named NIGHT,
On a black throne reigns upright,
I have wandered home but newly
From this ultimate dim Thule.

Dreams

Oh! that my young life were a lasting dream!
My spirit not awakening, till the beam
Of an Eternity should bring the morrow.
Yes! though that long dream were of hopeless sorrow,
'Twere better than the cold reality
Of waking life, to him whose heart must be,
And hath been still, upon the lovely earth,
A chaos of deep passion, from his birth.
But should it be—that dream eternally
Continuing—as dreams have been to me
In my young boyhood—should it thus be given,
'Twere folly still to hope for higher Heaven.
For I have revelled when the sun was bright
I' the summer sky, in dreams of living light
And loveliness—have left my very heart
Inclines of my imaginary apart[1]
From mine own home, with beings that have been
Of mine own thought—what more could I have seen?
'Twas once—and only once—and the wild hour
From my remembrance shall not pass—some power
Or spell had bound me—'twas the chilly wind
Came o'er me in the night, and left behind
Its image on my spirit—or the moon
Shone on my slumbers in her lofty noon
Too coldly—or the stars—howe'er it was
That dream was as that night-wind—let it pass.
I have been happy, though in a dream.
I have been happy—and I love the theme:

[1]In climes of mine imagining apart?—ED.

Dreams! in their vivid coloring of life
As in that fleeting, shadowy, misty strife
Of semblance with reality which brings
To the delirious eye, more lovely things
Of Paradise and Love—and all my own!—
Than young Hope in his sunniest hour hath known.

Eldorado

Gaily bedight,
A gallant knight,
In sunshine and in shadow,
Had journeyed long,
Singing a song,
In search of Eldorado.

But he grew old—
This knight so bold—
And o'er his heart a shadow
Fell as he found
No spot of ground
That looked like Eldorado.

And, as his strength
Failed him at length,
He met a pilgrim shadow—
"Shadow," said he,
"Where can it be—
This land of Eldorado?"

"Over the Mountains
Of the Moon,
Down the Valley of the Shadow,
Ride, boldly ride,"
The shade replied,—
"If you seek for Eldorado!"

An Enigma

"Seldom we find," says Solomon Don Dunce,
    "Half an idea in the profoundest sonnet.
Through all the flimsy things we see at once
    As easily as through a Naples bonnet—
    Trash of all trash!—how *can* a lady don it?
Yet heavier far than your Petrarchan stuff—
Owl-downy nonsense that the faintest puff
    Twirls into trunk-paper the while you con it."
And, veritably, Sol is right enough.
The general tuckermanities are arrant
Bubbles—ephemeral and *so* transparent—
    But *this* is, now,—you may depend upon it—
Stable, opaque, immortal—all by dint
Of the dear names that lie concealed within 't.

Eulalie

I dwelt alone
In a world of moan,
And my soul was a stagnant tide,
Till the fair and gentle Eulalie became my blushing bride—
Till the yellow-haired young Eulalie became my smiling
bride.

Ah, less—less bright
The stars of night
Than the eyes of the radiant girl!
And never a flake
That the vapor can make
With the moon-tints of purple and pearl,
Can vie with the modest Eulalie's most unregarded curl—
Can compare with the bright-eyed Eulalie's most humble
and careless curl.

Now Doubt—now Pain
Come never again,
For her soul gives me sigh for sigh,
And all day long
Shines, bright and strong,
Astarté within the sky,
While ever to her dear Eulalie upturns her matron eye—
While ever to her young Eulalie upturns her violet eye.

Evening Star

'Twas noontide of summer,
    And midtime of night,
And stars, in their orbits,
    Shone pale, through the light
Of the brighter, cold moon.
    'Mid planets her slaves,
Herself in the Heavens,
    Her beam on the waves.

    I gazed awhile
    On her cold smile;
Too cold—too cold for me—
    There passed, as a shroud,
    A fleecy cloud,
And I turned away to thee,
    Proud Evening Star,
    In thy glory afar
And dearer thy beam shall be;
    For joy to my heart
    Is the proud part
Thou bearest in Heaven at night,
    And more I admire
    Thy distant fire,
Than that colder, lowly light.

To F—

Beloved! amid the earnest woes
    That crowd around my earthly path—
(Drear path, alas! where grows
Not even one lonely rose)—
    My soul at least a solace hath
In dreams of thee, and therein knows
An Eden of bland repose.

And thus thy memory is to me
    Like some enchanted far-off isle
In some tumultuous sea—
Some ocean throbbing far and free
    With storms—but where meanwhile
Serenest skies continually
    Just o'er that one bright island smile.

To F—S S. O—D

Thou wouldst be loved—then let thy heart
    From its present pathway part not!
Being every thing which now thou art,
    Be nothing which thou art not.
So with the world thy gentle ways,
    Thy grace, thy more than beauty,
Shall be an endless theme of praise
    And love—a simple duty.

Fairy-Land

Dim vales—and shadowy floods—
And cloudy-looking woods,
Whose forms we can't discover
For the tears that drip all over.
Huge moons there wax and wane—
Again—again—again—
Every moment of the night
Forever changing places—
And they put out the star-light
With the breath from their pale faces.
About twelve by the moon-dial
One more filmy than the rest
(A kind which, upon trial,
They have found to be the best)
Comes down—still down—and down
With its centre on the crown
Of a mountain's eminence,
While its wide circumference
In easy drapery falls
Over hamlets, over halls,
Wherever they may be—
O'er the strange woods—o'er the sea—
Over spirits on the wing
Over every drowsy thing—
And buries them up quite
In a labyrinth of light—
And then, how deep!—Oh, deep!
Is the passion of their sleep.
In the morning they arise,
And their moony covering

Is soaring in the skies,
With the tempests as they toss,
Like——almost any thing—
Or a yellow Albatross.
They use that moon no more
For the same end as before—
Videlicet a tent
Which I think extravagant:
Its atomies, however,
Into a shower dissever,
Of which those butterflies,
Of earth, who seek the skies,
And so come down again
(Never-contended things!)
Have brought a specimen
Upon their quivering wings.

"The Happiest Day"

I

The happiest day—the happiest hour
   My seared and blighted heart hath known,
The highest hope of pride and power,
   I feel hath flown.

II

Of power! said I? Yes! such I ween
   But they have vanished long, alas!
The visions of my youth have been—
   But let them pass.

III

And pride, what have I now with thee?
   Another brow may ev'n inherit
The venom thou hast poured on me—
   Be still my spirit!

IV

The happiest day—the happiest hour
   Mine eyes shall see—have ever seen
The brightest glance of pride and power
   I feel have been:

V

But were that hope of pride and power
  Now offered with the pain
Ev'n *then* I felt—that brightest hour
  I would not live again:

VI

For on its wings was dark alloy
  And as it fluttered—fell
An essence—powerful to destroy
  A soul that knew it well.

The Haunted Palace

In the greenest of our valleys
    By good angels tenanted,
Once a fair and stately palace—
    Radiant palace—reared its head.
In the monarch Thought's dominion—
    It stood there!
Never seraph spread a pinion
    Over fabric half so fair!

Banners yellow, glorious, golden,
    On its roof did float and flow,
(This—all this—was in the olden
    Time long ago,)
And every gentle air that dallied,
    In that sweet day,
Along the ramparts plumed and pallid,
    A wingèd odor went away.

Wanderers in that happy valley,
    Through two luminous windows, saw
Spirits moving musically,
    To a lute's well-tuned law,
Round about a throne where, sitting
    (Porphyrogene!)
In state his glory well befitting,
    The ruler of the realm was seen.

And all with pearl and ruby glowing
    Was the fair palace-door,
Through which came flowing, flowing, flowing,
    And sparkling evermore,

A troop of Echoes, whose sweet duty
        Was but to sing,
In voices of surpassing beauty,
        The wit and wisdom of their king

But evil things, in robes of sorrow,
        Assailed the monarch's high estate.
(Ah, let us mourn!—for never morrow
        Shall dawn upon him desolate!)
And round about his home, the glory
        That blushed and bloomed
Is but a dim-remembered story
        Of the old time entombed.

And travellers now, within that valley,
        Through the red-litten windows see
Vast forms, that move fantastically
        To a discordant melody,
While, like a ghastly rapid river,
        Through the pale door
A hideous throng rush out forever
        And laugh—but smile no more.

To Helen

Helen, thy beauty is to me
   Like those Nicean barks of yore,
That gently, o'er a perfumed sea,
   The weary, way-worn wanderer bore
   To his own native shore.

On desperate seas long wont to roam,
   Thy hyacinth hair, thy classic face,
Thy Naiad airs have brought me home
   To the glory that was Greece
And the grandeur that was Rome.

Lo! in yon brilliant window-niche
   How statue-like I see thee stand!
   The agate lamp within thy hand,
Ah! Psyche, from the regions which
   Are Holy Land!

To Helen[1]

I saw thee once—once only—years ago;
I must not say *how* many—but *not* many.
It was a July midnight; and from out
A full-orbed moon, that, like thine own soul, soaring,
Sought a precipitate pathway up through heaven,
There fell a silvery-silken veil of light,
With quietude, and sultriness, and slumber,
Upon the upturn'd faces of a thousand
Roses that grew in an enchanted garden,
Where no wind dared to stir, unless on tiptoe—
Fell on the upturn'd faces of these roses
That gave out, in return for the love-light,
Their odorous souls in an ecstatic death—
Fell on the upturn'd faces of these roses
That smiled and died in this parterre, enchanted
By thee, and by the poetry of thy presence.

Clad all in white, upon a violet bank
I saw thee half reclining; while the moon
Fell on the upturn'd faces of the roses,
And on thine own, upturn'd—alas, in sorrow!

Was it not Fate that, on this July midnight—
Was it not Fate (whose name is also Sorrow),
That bade me pause before that garden-gate,
To breathe the incense of those slumbering roses?
No footsteps stirred; the hated world all slept,
Save only thee and me. (Oh, Heaven!—oh, God!
How my heart beats in coupling those two words!)

---

[1]This poem was written for Mrs. Sarah Helen Whitman.—ED.

Save only thee and me. I paused—I looked—
And in an instant all things disappeared.
(Ah, bear in mind this garden was enchanted!)

The pearly lustre of the moon went out;
The mossy banks and the meandering paths,
The happy flowers and the repining trees,
Were seen no more: the very roses' odors
Died in the arms of the adoring airs.
All—all expired save thee—save less than thou:
Save only the divine light in thine eyes—
Save but the soul in thine uplifted eyes.
I saw but them—they were the world to me.
I saw but them—saw only them for hours—
Saw only them until the moon went down.
What wild heart-histories seemed to lie enwritten
Upon those crystalline, celestial spheres!
How dark a woe! yet how sublime a hope!
How silently serene a sea of pride!
How daring an ambition! yet how deep—
How fathomless a capacity for love!

But now, at length, dear Dian sank from sight,
Into a western couch of thunder-cloud;
And thou, a ghost, amid the entombing trees
Didst glide away. *Only thine eyes remained.*
They *would not* go—they never yet have gone.
Lighting my lonely pathway home that night,
They have not left me (as my hopes have) since.

They follow me—they lead me through the years.
They are my ministers—yet I their slave.
Their office is to illumine and enkindle—
My duty, *to be saved* by their bright light,
And purified in their electric fire,
And sanctified in their Elysian fire.
They fill my soul with Beauty (which is Hope),
And are far up in heaven—the stars I kneel to
In the sad, silent watches of my night;
While even in the meridian glare of day
I see them still—two sweetly scintillant
Venuses, unextinguished by the sun!

Hymn

At morn—at noon—at twilight dim—
Maria! thou hast heard my hymn!
In joy and woe—in good and ill—
Mother of God, be with me still!
When the Hours flew brightly by,
And not a cloud obscured the sky,
My soul, lest it should truant be,
Thy grace did guide to thine and thee;
Now, when storms of Fate o'ercast
Darkly my Present and my Past,
Let my Future radiant shine
With sweet hopes of thee and thine!

Hymn to Aristogeiton
and Harmodius

Translation from the Greek

I

Wreathed in myrtle, my sword I'll conceal
 Like those champions devoted and brave,
When they plunged in the tyrant their steel,
 And to Athens deliverance gave.

II

Beloved heroes! your deathless souls roam
 In the joy breathing isles of the blest;
Where the mighty of old have their home—
 Where Achilles and Diomed rest.

III

In fresh myrtle my blade I'll entwine,
 Like Harmodius, the gallant and good,
When he made at the tutelar shrine
 A libation of Tyranny's blood.

IV

Ye deliverers of Athens from shame!
 Ye avengers of Liberty's wrongs!
Endless ages shall cherish your fame,
 Embalmed in their echoing songs!

Imitation

A dark unfathomed tide
Of interminable pride—
A mystery, and a dream,
Should my early life seem;
I say that dream was fraught
With a wild and waking thought
Of beings that have been,
Which my spirit hath not seen,
Had I let them pass me by,
With a dreaming eye!
Let none of earth inherit
That vision on my spirit;
Those thoughts I would control,
As a spell upon his soul:
For that bright hope at last
And that light time have past,
And my worldly rest hath gone
With a sigh as it passed on:
I care not though it perish
With a thought I then did cherish.

To Isadore

I

Beneath the vine-clad eaves,
　　　Whose shadows fall before
　　　Thy lowly cottage door—
Under the lilac's tremulous leaves—
Within thy snowy claspèd hand
　　　The purple flowers it bore.
Last eve in dreams, I saw thee stand,
Like queenly nymphs from Fairy-land—
Enchantress of the flowery wand,
　　　Most beauteous Isadore!

II

And when I bade the dream
　　　Upon thy spirit flee,
　　　Thy violet eyes to me
Upturned, did overflowing seem
With the deep, untold delight
　　　Of Love's serenity;
Thy classic brow, like lilies white
And pale as the Imperial Night
Upon her throne, with stars bedight,
　　　Enthralled my soul to thee!

III

Ah! ever I behold
　　Thy dreamy, passionate eyes,
　　Blue as the languid skies
Hung with the sunset's fringe of gold;
Now strangely clear thine image grows,
　　And olden memories
Are startled from their long repose
Like shadows on the silent snows
When suddenly the night-wind blows
　　Where quiet moonlight lies.

IV

Like music heard in dreams,
　　Like strains of harps unknown,
　　Of birds forever flown—
Audible as the voice of streams
That murmur in some leafy dell,
　　I hear thy gentlest tone,
And Silence cometh with her spell
Like that which on my tongue doth dwell,
When tremulous in dreams I tell
　　My love to thee alone!

Israfel [1]

In Heaven a spirit doth dwell
"Whose heart-strings are a lute";
None sing so wildly well
As the angel Israfel,
And the giddy stars (so legends tell)
Ceasing their hymns, attend the spell
    Of his voice, all mute.

Tottering above
    In her highest noon,
    The enamored moon
Blushes with love,
    While, to listen, the red levin
    (With the rapid Pleiads, even,
    Which were seven)
    Pauses in Heaven.

And they say (the starry choir
    And the other listening things)
That Israfeli's fire
Is owing to that lyre
    By which he sits and sings—
The trembling living wire
    Of those unusual strings.

But the skies that angel trod,
    Where deep thoughts are a duty—
Where Love's a grown-up God—
    Where the Houri glances are

[1] And the angel Israfel, whose heart-strings are a lute, and who has the sweetest voice of all God's creatures.—KORAN.

Imbued with all the beauty
    Which we worship in a star.

Therefore, thou art not wrong,
    Israfeli, who despisest
An unimpassioned song;
To thee the laurels belong,
Best bard, because the wisest!
Merrily live, and long!

The ecstasies above
    With thy burning measures suit—
Thy grief, thy joy, thy hate, thy love,
    With the fervor of thy lute—
    Well may the stars be mute!

Yes, Heaven is thine; but this
    Is a world of sweets and sours;
    Our flowers are merely—flowers,
And the shadow of thy perfect bliss
    Is the sunshine of ours.

If I could dwell
Where Israfel
    Hath dwelt, and he where I,
He might not sing so wildly well
    A mortal melody,
While a bolder note than this might swell
    From my lyre within the sky.

The Lake—to —

In spring of youth it was my lot
To haunt of the wide world a spot
The which I could not love the less—
So lovely was the loneliness
Of a wild lake, with black rock bound,
And the tall pines that towered around.

But when the Night had thrown her pall
Upon that spot, as upon all,
And the mystic wind went by
Murmuring in melody—
Then—ah! then I would awake
To the terror of the lone lake.

Yet that terror was not fright,
But a tremulous delight—
A feeling not the jewelled mine
Could teach or bribe me to define—
Nor Love—although the Love were thine.

Death was in that poisonous wave,
And in its gulf a fitting grave
For him who thence could solace bring
To his lone imagining—
Whose solitary soul could make
An Eden of that dim lake.

Lenore

Ah, broken is the golden bowl! the spirit flown forever!
Let the bell toll!—a saintly soul floats on the Stygian river;
And, Guy De Vere, hast *thou* no tear?—weep now or never
    more!
See on yon drear and rigid bier low lies thy love, Lenore!
Come! let the burial rite be read—the funeral song be
    sung!—
An anthem for the queenliest dead that ever died so young—
A dirge for her the doubly dead in that she died so young.

"Wretches! ye loved her for her wealth and hated her for
    her pride,
And when she fell in feeble health, ye blessed her—that she
    died!
How *shall* the ritual, then, be read?—the requiem how be
    sung
By you—by yours, the evil eye,—by yours, the slanderous
    tongue
That did to death the innocence that died, and died so
    young?"

Peccavimus; but rave not thus! and let a Sabbath song
Go up to God so solemnly the dead may feel no wrong!
The sweet Lenore hath "gone before," with Hope, that flew
    beside,
Leaving thee wild for the dear child that should have been
    thy bride—
For her, the fair and *debonnaire,* that now so lowly lies,
The life upon her yellow hair but not within her eyes—
The life still there, upon her hair—the death upon her eyes.

Avaunt! to-night my heart is light. No dirge will I upraise,
But waft the angel on her flight with a pæan of old days!
Let *no* bell toll!—lest her sweet soul, amid its hallowed
   mirth,
Should catch the note, as it doth float up from the damned
   Earth.
To friends above, from fiends below, the indignant ghost is
   riven—
From Hell unto a high estate far up within the Heaven—
From grief and groan, to a golden throne, beside the King
   of Heaven.

To M. L. S—[1]

Of all who hail thy presence as the morning—
Of all to whom thine absence is the night—
The blotting utterly from out high heaven
The sacred sun—of all who, weeping, bless thee
Hourly for hope—for life—ah! above all,
For the resurrection of deep-buried faith
In Truth—in Virtue—in Humanity—
Of all who, on Despair's unhallowed bed
Lying down to die, have suddenly arisen
At thy soft-murmured words, "Let there be light!"
At the soft-murmured words that were fulfilled
In the seraphic glancing of thine eyes—
Of all who owe thee most—whose gratitude
Nearest resembles worship—oh, remember
The truest—the most fervently devoted,
And think that those weak lines are written by him—
By him who, as he pens them, thrills to think
His spirit is communing with an angel's.

[1]Mrs. Marie Louise Shew.

To My Mother

Because I feel that, in the heavens above,
    The angels, whispering to one another,
Can find, among their burning terms of love,
    None so devotional as that of "Mother,"
Therefore by that dear name I long have called you,
    You who are more than mother unto me,
And fill my heart of hearts, where Death installed you,
    In setting my Virginia's spirit free.
My mother—my own mother, who died early,
    Was but the mother of myself; but you
Are mother to the one I loved so dearly,
    And thus are dearer than the mother I knew
By that infinity with which my wife
Was dearer to my soul than its soul-life.

To One in Paradise

Thou wast that all to me, love,
　　For which my soul did pine—
A green isle in the sea, love,
　　A fountain and a shrine,
All wreathed with fairy fruits and flowers,
　　And all the flowers were mine.

Ah, dream too bright to last!
　　Ah, starry Hope! that didst arise
But to be overcast!
　　A voice from out the Future cries,
"On! on!"—but o'er the Past
　　(Dim gulf!) my spirit hovering lies
Mute, motionless, aghast!

For, alas! alas! with me
　　The light of Life is o'er!
　　"No more—no more—no more—"
(Such language holds the solemn sea
　　To the sands upon the shore)
Shall bloom the thunder-blasted tree,
　　Or the stricken eagle soar!

And all my days are trances,
　　And all my nightly dreams
Are where thy dark eye glances,
　　And where thy footstep gleams—
In what ethereal dances,
　　By what eternal streams.

A Pæan

I

How shall the burial rite be read?
   The solemn song be sung?
The requiem for the loveliest dead,
   That ever died so young?

II

Her friends are gazing on her,
   And on her gaudy bier,
And weep!—oh! to dishonor
   Dead beauty with a tear!

III

They loved her for her wealth—
   And they hated her for her pride—
But she grew in feeble health,
   And they *love* her—that she died.

IV

They tell me (while they speak
   Of her "costly broider'd pall")
That my voice is growing weak—
   That I should not sing at all—

V

Or, that my tone should be
    Tun'd to such solemn song
So mournfully—so mournfully,
    That the dead may feel no wrong.

VI

But she is gone above,
    With young Hope at her side,
And I am drunk with love
    Of the dead, who is my bride.—

VII

Of the dead—dead who lies
    All perfum'd there,
With the death upon her eyes,
    And the life upon her hair.

VIII

Thus on the coffin loud and long
    I strike—the murmur sent
Through the gray chambers to my song
    Shall be the accompaniment.

IX

Thou diedst in thy life's June—
 But thou didst not die too fair:
Thou didst not die too soon,
 Nor with too calm an air.

X

From more than friends on earth,
 Thy life and love are riven,
To join the untainted mirth
 Of more than thrones in heaven.—

XI

Therefore, to thee this night
 I will no requiem raise,
But waft thee on thy flight,
 With a Pæan of old days.

Scenes From "Politian"

An Unpublished Drama

I

Rome.—*A Hall in a Palace. Alessandra and Castiglione.*

ALESSANDRA. Thou art sad, Castiglione.

CASTIGLIONE. Sad!—not I.
    Oh, I'm the happiest, happiest man in Rome!
    A few days more, thou knowest, my Alessandra,
    Will make thee mine. Oh, I am very happy!

ALESS. Methinks thou hast a singular way of showing
    Thy happiness!—what ails thee, cousin of mine?
    Why didst thou sigh so deeply?

CAS. Did I sigh?
    I was not conscious of it. It is a fashion,
    A silly—a most silly fashion I have
    When I am *very* happy. Did I sigh?   *(Sighing.)*

ALESS. Thou didst. Thou are not well. Thou hast indulged
    Too much of late, and I am vexed to see it.
    Late hours and wine, Castiglione,—these
    Will ruin thee! thou art already altered—
    Thy looks are haggard—nothing so wears away
    The constitution as late hours and wine.

CAS. *(Musing.)* Nothing, fair cousin, nothing—not even
      deep sorrow—
    Wears it away like evil hours and wine.
    I will amend.

ALESS. Do it! I would have thee drop
    Thy riotous company, too—fellows low born—
    Ill suit the like with old Di Broglio's heir
    And Alessandra's husband.

CAS. I will drop them.

ALESS. Thou wilt—thou must. Attend thou also more
    To thy dress and equipage—they are over plain
    For thy lofty rank and fashion—much depends
    Upon appearances.

CAS. I'll see to it.

ALESS. Then see to it!—pay more attention, sir,
    To a becoming carriage—much thou wantest
    In dignity.

CAS. Much, much, oh, much I want
    In proper dignity.

ALESS. *(Haughtily.)* Thou mockest me, sir!

CAS. *(Abstractedly.)* Sweet, gentle Lalage!

ALESS. Heard I aright?
    I speak to him—he speaks of Lalage!
    Sir Count! *(Places her hand on his shoulder.)* What art thou
        dreaming? he's not well!
    What ails thee, sir?

CAS. *(Starting.)* Cousin! fair cousin!—madam!
    I crave thy pardon—indeed I am not well—
    Your hand from off my shoulder, if you please.
    This air is most oppressive!—Madam—the Duke!

    Enter Di Broglio.

DI BROGLIO. My son, I've news for thee!—hey?—what's
   the matter?
   (Observing Alessandra.)
   I' the pouts? Kiss her, Castiglione! kiss her,
   You dog! and make it up, I say, this minute!
   I've news for you both. Politian is expected
   Hourly in Rome—Politian, Earl of Leicester!
   We'll have him at the wedding. 'Tis his first visit
   To the imperial city.

ALESS. What! Politian
   Of Britain, Earl of Leicester?

DI BROG. The same, my love.
   We'll have him at the wedding. A man quite young
   In years, but gray in fame. I have not seen him,
   But Rumor speaks of him as of a prodigy
   Pre-eminent in arts, and arms, and wealth,
   And high descent. We'll have him at the wedding.

ALESS. I have heard much of this Politian.
   Gay, volatile, and giddy—is he not?
   And little given to thinking.

DI BROG. Far from it, love.
   No branch, they say, of all philosophy
   So deep abstruse he has not mastered it.
   Learned as few are learned.

ALESS. 'Tis very strange!
   I have known men have seen Politian
   And sought his company. They speak of him
   As of one who entered madly into life,
   Drinking the cup of pleasure to the dregs.

CAS. Ridiculous! Now *I* have seen Politian
And know him well—nor learned nor mirthful he.
He is a dreamer and a man shut out
From common passions.

DI BROG Children, we disagree.
Let us go forth and taste the fragrant air
Of the garden. Did I dream, or did I hear
Politian was a *melancholy* man?   *(Exeunt.)*

II

ROME.—*A Lady's apartment, with a window open and looking
into a garden. Lalage, in deep mourning, reading at a table on which
lie some books and a hand mirror. In the background Jacinta (a servant
maid) leans carelessly upon a chair.*

LALAGE. Jacinta! is it thou?

JACINTA. *(Pertly.)* Yes, ma'am, I'm here.

LAL. I did not know, Jacinta, you were in waiting.
Sit down!—let not my presence trouble you—
Sit down!—for I am humble, most humble.

JAC. *(Aside.)* 'Tis time.
      *(Jacinta seats herself in a side-long manner upon the chair,
      resting her elbows upon the back, and regarding her mistress
      with a contemptuous look. Lalage continues to read.)*

LAL. "It in another climate, so he said,
Bore a bright golden flower, but not i' this soil!"
      (Pauses—turns over some leaves, and resumes.)
"No lingering winters there, nor snow, nor shower—
But Ocean ever to refresh mankind

Breathes the shrill spirit of the western wind."
Oh, beautiful!—most beautiful!—how like
To what my fevered soul doth dream of heaven!
O happy land! *(Pauses.)* She died!—the maiden died!
O still more happy maiden who couldst die!
Jacinta!

    (Jacinta returns no answer, and Lalage presently resumes.)
Again!—a similar tale
Told of a beauteous dame beyond the sea!
Thus speaketh one Ferdinand in the words of the play—
"She died full young"—one Bossola answers him—
"I think not so—her infelicity
Seemed to have years too many."—Ah, luckless lady!
Jacinta! *(Still no answer.)*

    Here's a far sterner story,
But like—oh, very like in its despair—
Of that Egyptian queen, winning so easily
A thousand hearts—losing at length her own.
She died. Thus endeth the history—and her maids
Lean over her and weep—two gentle maids
With gentle names—Eiros and Charmion!
Rainbow and Dove!——Jacinta!

JAC. *(Pettishly.)* Madam, what *is* it?

LAL. Wilt thou, my good Jacinta, be so kind
    As go down in the library and bring me
    The Holy Evangelists.

JAC. Pshaw! *(Exit.)*

LAL. If there be balm
    For the wounded spirit in Gilead it is there!
    Dew in the night-time of my bitter trouble

Will there be found—"dew sweeter far than that
Which hangs like chains of pearl on Hermon Hill."

(Re-enter Jacinta, and throws a volume on the table.)

There, ma'am, 's the book. Indeed she is very
    troublesome.   *(Aside.)*

LAL. *(Astonished.)* What didst thou say, Jacinta? Have I done
    aught
    To grieve thee or to vex thee?—I am sorry.
    For thou hast served me long and ever been
    Trustworthy and respectful. *(Resumes her reading.)*

JAC. I can't believe
    She has any more jewels—no—no—she gave me all.
                               (Aside.)

LAL. What didst thou say, Jacinta? Now I bethink me
    Thou hast not spoken lately of thy wedding.
    How fares good Ugo?—and when is it to be?
    Can I do aught?—is there no farther aid
    Thou needest, Jacinta?

JAC. Is there no *farther* aid!
    That's meant for me. *(Aside.)* I'm sure, Madame, you
    need not
    Be always throwing those jewels in my teeth.

LAL. Jewels? Jacinta,—now indeed, Jacinta,
    I thought not of the jewels.

JAC. Oh! perhaps not!
    But then I might have sworn it. After all,
    There's Ugo says the ring is only paste,
    For he's sure the Count Castiglione never

Would have given a real diamond to such as you;
And at the best I'm certain, madam, you cannot
Have use for jewels *now*. But I might have sworn it.

(Exit.)

(Lalage bursts into tears and leans her head upon the table—after a short pause raises it.)

LAL. Poor Lalage!—and is it come to this?
Thy servant maid!—but courage!—'tis but a viper
Whom thou hast cherished to sting thee to the soul!
(Taking up the mirror.)
Ha! here at least's a friend—too much a friend
In earlier days—a friend will not deceive thee.
Fair mirror and true! now tell me (for thou canst)
A tale—a pretty tale—and heed thou not
Though it be rife with woe. It answers me.
It speaks of sunken eyes, and wasted cheeks,
And Beauty long deceased—remembers me
Of Joy departed—Hope, the Seraph Hope,
Inurned and entombed!—now, in a tone
Low, sad, and solemn, but most audible,
Whispers of early grave untimely yawning
For ruined maid. Fair mirror and true!—thou liest not!
Thou hast no end to gain—no heart to break—
Castiglione lied who said he loved——
Thou true—he false!—false!—false!
(While she speaks, a monk enters her apartment, and approaches unobserved.)

MONK. Refuge thou hast,
Sweet daughter! in Heaven. Think of eternal things!
Give up thy soul to penitence, and pray!

LAL. *(Arising hurriedly.)* I cannot pray!—My soul is at war
 with God!
The frightful sounds of merriment below
Disturb my senses—go! I cannot pray—
The sweet airs from the garden worry me!
Thy presence grieves me—go!—thy priestly raiment
Fills me with dread—thy ebony crucifix
With horror and awe!

MONK. Think of thy precious soul!

LAL. Think of my early days!—think of my father
And mother in Heaven! think of our quiet home,
And the rivulet that ran before the door!
Think of my little sisters!—think of them!
And think of me!—think of my trusting love
And confidence—his vows—my ruin—think—think
Of my unspeakable misery!——begone!
Yet stay! yet stay!—what was it thou saidst of prayer
And penitence? Didst thou not speak of faith
And vows before the throne?

MONK. I did.

LAL. 'Tis well.
There *is* a vow were fitting should be made—
A sacred vow, imperative and urgent,
A solemn vow!

MONK. Daughter, this zeal is well!

LAL. Father, this zeal is any thing but well!
Hast thou a crucifix fit for this thing!
A crucifix whereon to register
This sacred vow? *(He hands her his own:)*

Not that—oh! no!—no!—no! *(Shuddering.)*
Not that! Not that!—I tell thee, holy man,
Thy raiments and thy ebony cross affright me!
Stand back! I have a crucifix myself,—
I have a crucifix! Methinks 'twere fitting
The deed—the vow—the symbol of the deed—
And the deed's register should tally, father!
    (Draws a cross-handled dagger and raises it on high.)
Behold the cross wherewith a vow like mine
Is written in Heaven!

MONK. Thy words are madness, daughter,
And speak a purpose unholy—thy lips are livid—
Thine eyes are wild—tempt not the wrath divine!
Pause ere too late!—oh, be not—be not rash!
Swear not the oath—oh, swear it not!

LAL. 'Tis sworn!

III

An apartment in a palace. Politian and Baldazzar.

BALDAZZAR. Arouse thee now, Politian!
Thou must not—nay, indeed, indeed, thou shalt not
Give way unto these humors. Be thyself!
Shake off the idle fancies that beset thee,
And live, for now thou diest!

POLITIAN. Not so, Baldazzar!
Surely I live.

BAL. Politian, it doth grieve me
To see thee thus.

POL. Baldazzar, it doth grieve me
　　To give thee cause for grief, my honored friend.
　　Command me, sir! what wouldst thou have me do?
　　At thy behest I will shake off that nature
　　Which from my forefathers I did inherit,
　　Which with my mother's milk I did imbibe,
　　And be no more Politian, but some other.
　　Command me, sir!

BAL. To the field then—to the field—
　　To the senate or the field.

POL. Alas! alas!
　　There is an imp would follow me even there!
　　There is an imp *hath* followed me even there!
　　There is——what voice was that?

BAL. I heard it not.
　　I heard not any voice except thine own,
　　And the echo of thine own.

POL. Then I but dreamed.

BAL. Give not thy soul to dreams: the camp—the court
　　Befit thee—Fame awaits thee—Glory calls—
　　And her the trumpet-tongued thou wilt not hear
　　In hearkening to imaginary sounds
　　And phantom voices.

POL. It *is* a phantom voice!
　　Didst thou not hear it *then?*

BAL. I heard it not.

POL. Thou heardst it not!——Baldazzar, speak no more
　　To me, Politian, of thy camps and courts.

Oh! I am sick, sick, sick, even unto death,
Of the hollow and high-sounding vanities
Of the populous Earth! Bear with me yet a while!
We have been boys together—school-fellows—
And now are friends—yet shall not be so long—
For in the eternal city thou shalt do me
A kind and gentle office, and a Power—
A Power august, benignant, and supreme—
Shall then absolve thee of all farther duties
Unto thy friend.

BAL.   Thou speakest a fearful riddle
I *will* not understand.

POL.   Yet now as Fate
Approaches, and the Hours are breathing low,
The sands of Time are changed to golden grains,
And dazzle me, Baldazzar. Alas! alas!
I *cannot* die, having within my heart
So keen a relish for the beautiful
As has been kindled within it. Methinks the air
Is balmier now than it was wont to be—
Rich melodies are floating in the winds—
A rarer loveliness bedecks the earth—
And with a holier lustre the quiet moon
Sitteth in heaven.—Hist! hist! thou canst not say
Thou hearest not now, Baldazzar?

BAL.   Indeed I hear not.

POL.   Not hear it!—listen now—listen!—the faintest sound
And yet the sweetest that ear ever heard!
A lady's voice!—and sorrow in the tone!
Baldazzar, it oppresses me like a spell!

Again!—again!—how solemnly it falls
Into my heart of hearts! that eloquent voice
Surely I never heard—yet it were well
Had I but heard it with its thrilling tones
In earlier days!

BAL. I myself hear it now.
　　　Be still!—the voice, if I mistake not greatly,
Proceeds from yonder lattice—which you may see
Very plainly through the window—it belongs,
Does it not? unto this palace of the Duke.
The singer is undoubtedly beneath
The roof of his Excellency—and perhaps
Is even that Alessandra of whom he spoke
As the betrothed of Castiglione,
His son and heir.

POL. Be still!—it comes again!
　　　Voice　　　"And is thy heart so strong
　　　(very faintly.) As for to leave me thus
　　　　　　　　　Who hath loved thee so long
　　　　　　　　　In wealth and woe among?
　　　　　　　　　And is thy heart so strong
　　　　　　　　　As for to leave me thus?
　　　　　　　　　　　Say nay—say nay!"

BAL. The song is English, and I oft have heard it
In merry England—never so plaintively—
Hist! hist! it comes again!
　　　Voice　　　"Is it so strong
　　　(more loudly.) As for to leave me thus
　　　　　　　　　Who hath loved thee so long,
　　　　　　　　　In wealth and woe among?

And is thy heart so strong
        As for to leave me thus?
            Say nay—say nay!"

BAL. 'Tis hushed and all is still!

POL. All is not still.

BAL. Let us go down.

POL. Go down, Baldazzar, go!

BAL. The hour is growing late—the Duke awaits us,—
    Thy presence is expected in the hall
    Below. What ails thee, Earl Politian?
    Voice   "Who hath loved thee so long,
    (distinctly.) In wealth and woe among,
            And is thy heart so strong?
                Say nay—say nay!"

BAL. Let us descend!—'tis time. Politian, give
    These fancies to the wind. Remember, pray,
    Your bearing lately savored much of rudeness
    Unto the Duke. Arouse thee! and remember!

POL. Remember? I do. Lead on! I do remember.   *(Going.)*
    Let us descend. Believe me, I would give,
    Freely would give, the broad lands of my earldom
    To look upon the face hidden by yon lattice—
    "To gaze upon that veiled face, and hear
    Once more that silent tongue."

BAL. Let me beg you, sir,
    Descend with me—the Duke may be offended.
    Let us go down, I pray you.
    (Voice loudly.) Say nay!—say nay!

POL. *(Aside.)* 'Tis strange!—'tis very strange—methought
the voice
Chimed in with my desires and bade me stay!
(Approaching the window.)
Sweet voice! I heed thee, and will surely stay.
Now be this Fancy, by Heaven, or be it Fate,
Still will I not descend. Baldazzar, make
Apology unto the Duke for me;
I go not down to-night.

BAL. Your lordship's pleasure
Shall be attended to. Good-night, Politian.

POL. Good-night, my friend, good-night.

IV

The gardens of a palace—Moonlight. Lalage and Politian.

LALAGE. And dost thou speak of love
To *me,* Politian?—dost thou speak of love
To Lalage?—ah, woe!—ah, woe is me!
This mockery is most cruel—most cruel indeed!

POLITIAN. Weep not! oh, sob not thus!—thy bitter tears
Will madden me. Oh, mourn not, Lalage—
Be comforted! I know—I know it all,
And *still* I speak of love. Look at me, brightest,
And beautiful Lalage!—turn here thine eyes!
Thou askest me if I could speak of love,
Knowing what I know, and seeing what I have seen.
Thou askest me that—and thus I answer thee—
Thus on my bended knee I answer thee. *(Kneeling.)*
Sweet Lalage, *I love thee—love thee—love thee;*

Thro' good and ill—thro' weal and woe I *love thee.*
Not mother, with her first-born on her knee,
Thrills with intenser love than I for thee.
Not on God's altar, in any time or clime,
Burned there a holier fire than burneth now
Within my spirit for *thee.* And do I love?   *(Arising.)*
Even for thy woes I love thee—even for thy woes—
Thy beauty and thy woes.

LAL. Alas, proud Earl,
    Thou dost forget thyself, remembering me!
    How, in thy father's halls, among the maidens
    Pure and reproachless of thy princely line,
    Could the dishonored Lalage abide?
    Thy wife, and with a tainted memory—
    My seared and blighted name, how would it tally
    With the ancestral honors of thy house,
    And with thy glory?

POL. Speak not to me of glory!
    I hate—I loathe the name! I do abhor
    The unsatisfactory and ideal thing.
    Art thou not Lalage and I Politian?
    Do I not love—art thou not beautiful—
    What need we more? Ha! glory!—now speak not of it.
    By all I hold most sacred and most solemn—
    By all my wishes now—my fears hereafter—
    By all I scorn on earth and hope in heaven—
    There is no deed I would more glory in,
    Than in thy cause to scoff at this same glory
    And trample it under foot. What matters it—
    What matters it, my fairest, and my best,
    That we go down unhonored and forgotten

Into the dust—so we descend together?
Descend together—and then—and then perchance——

LAL. Why dost thou pause, Politian?

POL. And then perchance
　　Arise together, Lalage, and roam
　　The starry and quiet dwellings of the blest,
　　And still——

LAL. Why dost thou pause, Politian?

POL. And still *together—together*

LAL. Now, Earl of Leicester!
　　Thou *lovest* me, and in my heart of hearts
　　I feel thou lovest me truly

POL. Oh, Lalage!　　　　　　*(Throwing himself upon his knee.)*
　　And lovest thou *me*?

LAL. Hist! hush! within the gloom
　　Of yonder trees methought a figure past—
　　A spectral figure, solemn, and slow, and noiseless—
　　Like the grim shadow Conscience, solemn and noiseless.
　　　　　　　　　　　　(Walks across and returns.)
　　I was mistaken—'twas but a giant bough
　　Stirred by the autumn wind. Politian!

POL. My Lalage—my love! why art thou moved?
　　Why dost thou turn so pale? Not Conscience' self,
　　Far less a shadow which thou likenest to it,
　　Should shake the firm spirit thus. But the night wind
　　Is chilly—and these melancholy boughs
　　Throw over all things a gloom.

LAL. Politian!
    Thou speakest to me of love. Knowest thou the land
    With which all tongues are busy—a land new found—
    Miraculously found by one of Genoa—
    A thousand leagues within the golden west?
    A fairy land of flowers, and fruit, and sunshine,
    And crystal lakes, and over-arching forests,
    And mountains, around whose towering summits the
        winds
    Of Heaven untrammelled flow—which air to breathe
    Is Happiness now, and will be Freedom hereafter
    In days that are to come?

POL. Oh, wilt thou—wilt thou
    Fly to that Paradise—my Lalage, wilt thou
    Fly thither with me? There Care shall be forgotten,
    And Sorrow shall be no more, and Eros be all.
    And life shall then be mine, for I will live
    For thee, and in thine eyes—and thou shalt be
    No more a mourner—but the radiant Joys
    Shall wait upon thee, and the angel Hope
    Attend thee ever; and I will kneel to thee,
    And worship thee, and call thee my beloved,
    My all;—oh, wilt thou—wilt thou, Lalage,
    Fly thither with me?

LAL. A deed is to be done—
    Castiglione lives!

POL. And he shall die.   (Exit.)

LAL. (After a pause.) And—he—shall—die?——alas!
    Castiglione die? Who spoke the words?
    Where am I?—what was it he said?—Politian!

Thou *art* not gone—thou art not *gone,* Politian!
I feel thou art not gone—yet dare not look,
Lest I behold thee not; thou *couldst* not go
With those words upon thy lips—oh, speak to me!
And let me hear thy voice—one word—one word,
To say thou art not gone,—one little sentence,
To say how thou dost scorn—how thou dost hate
My womanly weakness. Ha! ha! thou *art* not gone—
Oh, speak to me! I *knew* thou wouldst not go!
I knew thou wouldst not, couldst not, *durst* not go.
Villain, thou *art* not gone—thou mockest me!
And thus I clutch thee—thus!——He is gone, he is
      gone—
Gone—gone. Where am I?——'tis well—'tis very well!
So that the blade be keen—the blow be sure,
'Tis well, 'tis *very* well—alas! alas!

V

The suburbs. Politian alone.

POLITIAN. This weakness grows upon me. I am faint,
      And much I fear me ill—it will not do
      To die ere I have lived!—Stay—stay thy hand,
      O Azrael, yet awhile!—Prince of the Powers
      Of Darkness and the Tomb, O pity me!
      O pity me! let me not perish now,
      In the budding of my Paradisal Hope!
      Give me to live yet—yet a little while:
      'Tis I who pray for life—I who so late
      Demanded but to die!—what sayeth the Count?

Enter Baldazzar

BALDAZZAR. That, knowing no cause of quarrel or of feud
    Between the Earl Politian and himself,
    He doth decline your cartel.

POL. What didst thou say?
    What answer was it you brought me, good Baldazzar?
    With what excessive fragrance the zephyr comes
    Laden from yonder bowers!—a fairer day,
    Or one more worthy Italy, methinks
    No mortal eyes have seen!—*what* said the Count?

BAL. That he, Castiglione, not being aware
    Of any feud existing, or any cause
    Of quarrel between your lordship and himself,
    Cannot accept the challenge.

POL. It is most true—
    All this is very true. When saw you, sir,
    When saw you now, Baldazzar, in the frigid
    Ungenial Britain which we left so lately,
    A heaven so calm as this—so utterly free
    From the evil taint of clouds?—and he did *say?*

BAL. No more, my lord, than I have told you, sir:
    The Count Castiglione will not fight,
    Having no cause for quarrel.

POL. Now this is true—
    All very true. Thou art my friend, Baldazzar,
    And I have not forgotten it—thou'lt do me
    A piece of service; wilt thou go back and say
    Unto this man, that I, the Earl of Leicester,
    Hold him a villain?—thus much, I prythee, say
    Unto the Count—it is exceeding just

He should have cause for quarrel.

BAL. My lord!—my friend!——

POL. *(Aside.)* 'Tis he—he comes himself! *(Aloud.)* Thou
    reasonest well.
I know what thou wouldst say—not send the message—
Well!—I will think of it—I will not send it.
Now prythee, leave me—hither doth come a person
With whom affairs of a most private nature
I would adjust.

BAL. I go—to-morrow we meet,
    Do we not?—at the Vatican.

POL. At the Vatican.

Enter Castiglione.

CAS. The Earl of Leicester here!

POL. I *am* the Earl of Leicester, and thou seest,
    dost thou not? that I am here.

CAS. My lord, some strange,
    Some singular mistake—misunderstanding—
Hath without doubt arisen: thou hast been urged
Thereby, in heat of anger, to address
Some words most unaccountable, in writing,
To me, Castiglione; the bearer being
Baldazzar, Duke of Surrey. I am aware
Of nothing which might warrant thee in this thing,
Having given thee no offence. Ha!—am I right?
'Twas a mistake?—undoubtedly—we all
Do err at times.

POL. Draw, villain, and prate no more!

CAS. Ha!—draw?—and villain? have at thee then at once,
Proud Earl!

POL. *(Drawing.)* Thus to the expiatory tomb,
Untimely sepulchre, I do devote thee
In the name of Lalage!

CAS. *(Letting fall his sword and recoiling to the extremity of the
stage.)* Of Lalage!
Hold off—thy sacred hand!—avaunt I say!
Avaunt—I will not fight thee—indeed I dare not.

POL. Thou wilt not fight with me, didst say, Sir Count?
Shall I be baffled thus?—now this is well;
Didst say thou darest not? Ha!

CAS. I dare not—dare not—
Hold off thy hand—with that beloved name
So fresh upon thy lips I will not fight thee—
I cannot—dare not.

POL. Now by my halidom
I do believe thee! coward, I do believe thee!

CAS. Ha! coward! this may not be!
*(Clutches his sword and staggers toward Politian, but his
purpose is changed before reaching him, and he falls upon
his knee at the feet of the Earl.)*
Alas! my lord,
It is—it is—most true. In such a cause
I am the veriest coward. Oh, pity me!

POL. *(Greatly softened.)* Alas! I do—indeed I pity thee.

CAS. And Lalage——

POL. *Scoundrel!—arise and die!*

CAS. It needeth not be—thus—thus—Oh, let me die
Thus on my bended knee! It were most fitting.
That in this deep humiliation I perish.
For in the fight I will not raise a hand
Against thee, Earl of Leicester. Strike thou home—
(Baring his bosom.)
Here is no let or hindrance to thy weapon—
Strike home. I will not fight thee.

POL. Now s'Death and Hell!
Am I not—am I not sorely—grievously tempted
To take thee at thy word? But mark me, sir:
Think not to fly me thus. Do thou prepare
For public insults in the streets—before
The eyes of the citizens. I'll follow thee—
Like an avenging spirit I'll follow thee
Even unto death. Before those whom thou lovest—
Before all Rome I'll taunt thee, villain,—I'll taunt thee,
Dost hear? with *cowardice*—thou *wilt* not fight me?
Thou liest! thou shalt! *(Exit.)*

CAS. Now this indeed is just!
Most righteous, and most just, avenging Heaven!

The Raven

Once upon a midnight dreary, while I pondered, weak and
   weary,
Over many a quaint and curious volume of forgotten lore—
While I nodded, nearly napping, suddenly there came a tapping,
As of some one gently rapping, rapping at my chamber
   door.
" 'Tis some visitor," I muttered, "tapping at my chamber
   door—
               Only this and nothing more."

Ah, distinctly I remember it was in the bleak December,
And each separate dying ember wrought its ghost upon the
   floor.
Eagerly I wished the morrow;—vainly I had sought to bor-
   row
From my books surcease of sorrow—sorrow for the lost Lenore—
For the rare and radiant maiden whom the angels name Lenore—
               Nameless here for evermore.

And the silken sad uncertain rustling of each purple curtain
Thrilled me—filled me with fantastic terrors never felt be-
   fore;
So that now, to still the beating of my heart, I stood repeat-
   ing:
" 'Tis some visitor entreating entrance at my chamber door—
Some late visitor entreating entrance at my chamber door;
               This it is and nothing more."

Presently my soul grew stronger; hesitating then no longer,
"Sir," said I, "or Madam, truly your forgiveness I implore;
But the fact is I was napping, and so gently you came rap-
ping,
And so faintly you came tapping, tapping at my chamber
door,
That I scarce was sure I heard you"—here I opened wide
the door;—
Darkness there and nothing more.

Deep into that darkness peering, long I stood there won-
dering, fearing,
Doubting, dreaming dreams no mortals ever dared to dream
before;
But the silence was unbroken, and the stillness gave no to-
ken,
And the only word there spoken was the whispered word,
"Lenore!"
This I whispered, and an echo murmured back the word,
"Lenore!"—
Merely this and nothing more.

Back into the chamber turning, all my soul within me
burning,
Soon again I heard a tapping something louder than before.
"Surely," said I, "surely that is something at my window lat-
tice;
Let me see, then, what thereat is, and this mystery explore—
Let my heart be still a moment, and this mystery explore;—
'Tis the wind and nothing more."

Open here I flung the shutter, when, with many a flirt and
flutter,
In there stepped a stately Raven of the saintly days of yore.
Not the least obeisance made he; not a minute stopped or
stayed he,
But, with mien of lord or lady, perched above my chamber
door—
Perched upon a bust of Pallas just above my chamber door—
Perched, and sat, and nothing more.

Then this ebony bird beguiling my sad fancy into smiling,
By the grave and stern decorum of the countenance it
wore,
"Though thy crest be shorn and shaven, thou," I said, "art
sure no craven,
Ghastly grim and ancient Raven wandering from the
Nightly shore—
Tell me what thy lordly name is on the Night's Plutonian
shore!"
Quoth the Raven, "Nevermore."

Much I marvelled this ungainly fowl to hear discourse so
plainly,
Though its answer little meaning—little relevancy bore;
For we cannot help agreeing that no living human being
Ever yet was blessed with seeing bird above his chamber
door—
Bird or beast upon the sculptured bust above his chamber
door,
With such name as "Nevermore."

But the Raven, sitting lonely on that placid bust, spoke only
That one word, as if his soul in that one word he did outpour.
Nothing farther then he uttered; not a feather then he fluttered—
Till I scarcely more than muttered: "Other friends have
 flown before—
On the morrow *he* will leave me as my Hopes have flown
 before."
                    Then the bird said, "Nevermore."

Startled at the stillness broken by reply so aptly spoken,
"Doubtless," said I, "what it utters is its only stock and
 store,
Caught from some unhappy master whom unmerciful Dis-
 aster
Followed fast and followed faster till his songs one burden
 bore—
Till the dirges of his Hope that melancholy burden bore
                    Of 'Never—nevermore.' "

But the Raven still beguiling all my sad soul into smiling,
Straight I wheeled a cushioned seat in front of bird and bust
 and door;
Then, upon the velvet sinking, I betook myself to linking
Fancy unto fancy, thinking what this ominous bird of yore—
What this grim, ungainly, ghastly, gaunt, and ominous bird
 of yore
                    Meant in croaking "Nevermore."

This I sat engaged in guessing, but no syllable expressing
To the fowl whose fiery eyes now burned into my bosom's
    core;
This and more I sat divining, with my head at ease reclining
On the cushion's velvet lining that the lamp-light gloated
    o'er,
But whose velvet violet lining with the lamp-light gloating
    o'er
                    She shall press, ah, nevermore!

Then, methought, the air grew denser, perfumed from an
    unseen censer
Swung by Seraphim whose foot-falls tinkled on the tufted
    floor.
"Wretch," I cried, "thy God hath lent thee—by these an-
    gels he hath sent thee
Respite—respite and nepenthe from thy memories of Le-
    nore!
Quaff, oh quaff this kind nepenthe and forget this lost Le-
    nore!"
                    Quoth the Raven, "Nevermore."

"Prophet!" said I, "thing of evil!—prophet still, if bird or
    devil!—
Whether Tempter sent, or whether tempest tossed thee here
    ashore,
Desolate, yet all undaunted, on this desert land enchanted—
On this home by Horror haunted,—tell me truly, I implore—
Is there—*is* there balm in Gilead?—tell me—tell me, I im-
    plore!"
                    Quoth the Raven, "Nevermore."

"Prophet!" said I, "thing of evil!—prophet still, if bird or
devil!
By that heaven that bends above us—by that God we both
adore—
Tell this soul with sorrow laden if, within the distant Aidenn,
It shall clasp a sainted maiden whom the angels name Lenore—
Clasp a rare and radiant maiden whom the angels name Lenore."
                                Quoth the Raven, "Nevermore."

"Be that word our sign of parting, bird or fiend!" I
shrieked, upstarting—
"Get thee back into the tempest and the Night's Plutonian
shore!
Leave no black plume as a token of that lie thy soul hath
spoken!
Leave my loneliness unbroken!—quit the bust above my door!
Take thy beak from out my heart, and take thy form from
off my door!"
                                Quoth the Raven, "Nevermore."

And the Raven, never flitting, still is sitting, still is sitting
On the pallid bust of Pallas just above my chamber door;
And his eyes have all the seeming of a demon's that is
dreaming,
And the lamp-light o'er him streaming throws his shadow
on the floor;
And my soul from out that shadow that lies floating on the
floor
                                Shall be lifted—nevermore!

To The River —

Fair river! in thy bright, clear flow
    Of crystal, wandering water,
Thou art an emblem of the glow
Of beauty—the unhidden heart—
The playful maziness of art
    In old Alberto's daughter;

But when within thy wave she looks—
    Which glistens then, and trembles—
Why, then, the prettiest of brooks
    Her worshipper resembles;
For in his heart, as in thy stream,
    Her image deeply lies—
His heart which trembles at the beam
    Of her soul-searching eyes.

Romance

Romance, who loves to nod and sing,
  With drowsy head and folded wing,
Among the green leaves as they shake
Far down within some shadowy lake
  To me a painted paroquet
Hath been—a most familiar bird—
  Taught me my alphabet to say,
To lisp my very earliest word
While in the wild wood I did lie,
A child—with a most knowing eye.

Of late, eternal Condor years
  So shake the very Heaven on high
  With tumult as they thunder by,
I have no time for idle cares
  Through gazing on the unquiet sky.
And when an hour with calmer wings
Its down upon my spirit flings—
That little time with lyre and rhyme
  To while away—forbidden things!
My heart would feel to be a crime
  Unless it trembled with the strings.

Silence

There are some qualities—some incorporate things,
     That have a double life, which thus is made
A type of that twin entity which springs
     From matter and light, evinced in solid and shade.
There is a twofold *Silence*—sea and shore—
     Body and soul. One dwells in lonely places,
     Newly with grass o'ergrown; some solemn graces,
Some human memories and tearful lore,
Render him terrorless: his name's "No More."
He is the corporate Silence: dread him not!
     No power hath he of evil in himself;
But should some urgent fate (untimely lot!)
     Bring thee to meet his shadow (nameless elf,
That haunteth the lone regions where hath trod
No foot of man), commend thyself to God.

The Sleeper

At midnight, in the month of June,
I stand beneath the mystic moon.
An opiate vapor, dewy, dim,
Exhales from out her golden rim,
And, softly dripping, drop by drop,
Upon the quiet mountain top,
Steals drowsily and musically
Into the universal valley.
The rosemary nods upon the grave;
The lily lolls upon the wave;
Wrapping the fog about its breast,
The ruin moulders into rest;
Looking like Lethe, see! the lake
A conscious slumber seems to take,
And would not, for the world, awake.
All Beauty sleeps!—and lo! where lies
(Her casement open to the skies)
Irene, with her Destinies!

Oh, lady bright! can it be right—
This window open to the night?
The wanton airs, from the tree-top,
Laughingly through the lattice drop—
The bodiless airs, a wizard rout,
Flit through thy chamber in and out,
And wave the curtain canopy
So fitfully—so carefully—
Above the closed and fringed lid
'Neath which thy slumb'ring soul lies hid,
That, o'er the floor and down the wall,

Like ghosts the shadows rise and fall!
Oh, lady dear, hast thou no fear?
Why and what art thou dreaming here?
Sure thou art come o'er far-off seas,
A wonder to these garden trees!
Strange is thy pallor! strange thy dress!
Strange, above all, thy length of tress,
And this all solemn silentness!

The lady sleeps! Oh, may her sleep,
Which is enduring, so be deep!
Heaven have her in its sacred keep!
This chamber changed for one more holy,
This bed for one more melancholy,
I pray to God that she may lie
Forever with unopened eye,
While the dim sheeted ghosts go by!

My love, she sleeps! Oh, may her sleep,
As it is lasting, so be deep!
Soft may the worms about her creep!
Far in the forest, dim and old,
For her may some tall vault unfold—
Some vault that oft hath flung its black
And winged panels fluttering back,
Triumphant, o'er the crested palls,
Of her grand family funerals—
Some sepulchre, remote, alone,
Against whose portal she hath thrown,

In childhood, many an idle stone—
Some tomb from out whose sounding door
She ne'er shall force an echo more,
Thrilling to think, poor child of sin!
It was the dead who groaned within.

Song

I saw thee on thy bridal day—
    When a burning blush came o'er thee,
Though happiness around thee lay,
    The world all love before thee:

And in thine eye a kindling light
    (Whatever it might be)
Was all on Earth my aching sight
    Of Loveliness could see.

That blush, perhaps, was maiden shame—
    As such it well may pass—
Though its glow hath raised a fiercer flame
    In the breast of him, alas!

Who saw thee on that bridal day,
    When that deep blush *would* come o'er thee,
Though happiness around thee lay,
    The world all love before thee.

Sonnet–To Science

Science! true daughter of Old Time thou art!
    Who alterest all things with thy peering eyes.
Why preyest thou thus upon the poet's heart,
    Vulture, whose wings are dull realities?
How should he love thee? or how deem thee wise?
    Who wouldst not leave him in his wandering
To seek for treasure in the jewelled skies,
    Albeit he soared with an undaunted wing?
Hast thou not dragged Diana from her car?
    And driven the Hamadryad from the wood
To seek a shelter in some happier star?
    Hast thou not torn the Naiad from her flood,
The Elfin from the green grass, and from me
The summer dream beneath the tamarind tree?

Spirits of the Dead

Thy soul shall find itself alone
'Mid dark thoughts of the gray tombstone—
Not one, of all the crowd, to pry
Into thine hour of secrecy.

Be silent in that solitude
   Which is not loneliness, for then
The spirits of the dead who stood
   In life before thee are again
In death around thee, and their will
Shall overshadow thee: be still.

The night, tho' clear, shall frown,
And the stars shall not look down
From their high thrones in the Heaven
With light like Hope to mortals given;
But their red orbs, without beam,
To thy weariness shall seem

As a burning and a fever
Which would cling to thee forever.
Now are thoughts thou shalt not banish—
Now are visions ne'er to vanish;
From thy spirit shall they pass
No more—like dew-drops from the grass.

The breeze—the breath of God—is still,
And the mist upon the hill
Shadowy—shadowy—yet unbroken,
Is a symbol and a token,—
How it hangs upon the trees,
A mystery of mysteries!

Tamerlane

Kind solace in a dying hour!
    Such, father, is not (now) my theme—
I will not madly deem that power
        Of Earth may shrive me of the sin
        Unearthly pride that revell'd in—
    I have no time to dote or dream:
You call it hope—that fire of fire!
It is but agony of desire:
If I *can* hope—O God! I can—
    Its fount is holier—more divine—
I would not call thee fool, old man,
    But, such is not a gift of thine.

Know thou the secret of a spirit
    Bow'd from its wild pride into shame.
O yearning heart! I did inherit
    Thy withering portion with the fame,
The searing glory which hath shone
Amid the Jewels of my throne,
Halo of Hell! and with a pain
Not Hell shall make me fear again—
O craving heart, for the lost flowers
And sunshine of my summer hours!
The undying voice of that dead time,
With its interminable chime,
Rings, in the spirit of a spell,
Upon thy emptiness—a knell.

I have not always been as now:
The fever'd diadem on my brow
    I claim'd and won usurpingly——

Hath not the same fierce heirdom given
　　Rome to the Cæsar—this to me?
　　　　The heritage of a kingly mind,
And a proud spirit which hath striven
　　　　Triumphantly with human kind.

On mountain soil I first drew life:
　　The mists of the Taglay have shed
　　Nightly their dews upon my head,
And I believe, the wingèd strife
And tumult of the headlong air
Have nestled in my very hair.

So late from Heaven—that dew—it fell
　　('Mid dreams of an unholy night)
Upon me with the touch of Hell,
　　While the red flashing of the light
From clouds that hung, like banners, o'er,
　　Appeared to my half-closing eye
　　The pageantry of monarchy,
And the deep trumpet-thunder's roar
　　Came hurriedly upon me, telling
　　　　Of human battle, where my voice,
　　My own voice, silly child!—was swelling
　　　　(Oh! how my spirit would rejoice,
And leap within me at the cry)
The battle-cry of Victory!

The rain came down upon my head
　　Unshelter'd—and the heavy wind
　　Rendered me mad and deaf and blind.

It was but man, I thought, who shed
    Laurels upon me: and the rush—
The torrent of the chilly air
    Gurgled within my ear the crush
Of empires—with the captive's prayer—
The hum of suitors—and the tone
Of flattery 'round a sovereign's throne.

My passions, from that hapless hour,
    Usurp'd a tyranny which men
Have deem'd, since I have reached to power,
      My innate nature—be it so:
    But, father, there liv'd one who, then,
Then—in my boyhood—when their fire
      Burn'd with a still intenser glow
(For passion must, with youth, expire)
    E'en *then* who knew this iron heart
    In woman's weakness had a part.

I have no words—alas!—to tell
The loveliness of loving well!
Nor would I now attempt to trace
The more than beauty of a face
Whose lineaments, upon my mind,
Are——shadows on th' unstable wind:
Thus I remember having dwelt
    Some page of early lore upon,
With loitering eye, till I have felt
The letters—with their meaning—melt
    To fantasies—with none.

Oh, she was worthy of all love!
      Love, as in infancy, was mine—
'Twas such as angel minds above
      Might envy; her young heart the shrine
On which my every hope and thought
      Were incense—then a goodly gift,
            For they were childish and upright—
Pure——as her young example taught;
      Why did I leave it, and, adrift,
            Trust to the fire within for light?

We grew in age—and love—together—
      Roaming the forest and the wild;
My breast her shield in wintry weather—
      And when the friendly sunshine smil'd.
And she would mark the opening skies,
I saw no Heaven—but in her eyes.

Young Love's first lesson is——the heart;
      For 'mid that sunshine and those smiles,
When, from our little cares apart,
      And laughing at her girlish wiles,
I'd throw me on her throbbing breast,
      And pour my spirit out in tears—
There was no need to speak the rest—
      No need to quiet any fears
Of her—who ask'd no reason why,
But turn'd on me her quiet eye!

Yet *more* than worthy of the love
My spirit struggled with, and strove,

When, on the mountain peak, alone,
Ambition lent it a new tone—
I had no being, but in thee:
    The world, and all it did contain
In the earth—the air—the sea—
    Its joy—its little lot of pain
That was new pleasure——the ideal,
    Dim, vanities of dreams by night—
And dimmer nothings which were real—
    (Shadows—and a more shadowy light!)
Parted upon their misty wings,
        And so, confusedly, became
        Thine image and—a name—a name!
Two separate—yet most intimate things.

I was ambitious—have you known
    The passion, father? You have not:
A cottager, I mark'd a throne
Of half the world as all my own,
    And murmur'd at such lowly lot—
But, just like any other dream,
    Upon the vapor of the dew
My own had past, did not the beam
    Of beauty which did while it thro'
The minute—the hour—the day—oppress
My mind with double loveliness.

We walk'd together on the crown
Of a high mountain which look'd down
Afar from its proud natural towers
    Of rock and forest on the hills—

The dwindled hills! begirt with bowers
And shouting with a thousand rills.

I spoke to her of power and pride,
But mystically—in such guise
That she might deem it nought beside
The moment's converse; in her eyes
I read, perhaps too carelessly,
A mingled feeling with my own;
The flush on her bright cheek to me
Seem'd to become a queenly throne
Too well that I should let it be
Light in the wilderness alone.

I wrapp'd myself in grandeur then,
And donn'd a visionary crown;
Yet it was not that Fantasy
Had thrown her mantle over me,
But that, among the rabble—men—
Lion ambition is chain'd down,
And crouches to a keeper's hand;
Not so in deserts where the grand—
The wild—the terrible conspire
With their own breath to fan his fire.

Look 'round thee now on Samarcand!
Is she not queen of Earth? her pride
Above all cities? in her hand
Their destinies? in all beside
Of glory which the world hath known,
Stands she not nobly and alone?

Falling, her veriest stepping-stone
Shall form the pedestal of a throne,—
And who her sovereign? Timour,—he
    Whom the astonished people saw
Striding o'er empires haughtily
    A diadem'd outlaw!

O human love! thou spirit given
On Earth of all we hope in Heaven!
Which fall'st into the soul like rain
Upon the Siroc-wither'd plain,
And, failing in thy power to bless,
But leav'st the heart a wilderness!
Idea! which bindest life around
With music of so strange a sound,
And beauty of so wild a birth,—
Farewell! for I have won the Earth.

When Hope, the eagle that tower'd, could see
    No cliff beyond him in the sky,
His pinions were bent droopingly,
    And homeward turn'd his soften'd eye.
'Twas sunset: when the sun will part
There comes a sullenness of heart
To him who still would look upon
The glory of the summer sun.
That soul will hate the ev'ning mist,
So often lovely, and will list
To the sound of the coming darkness (known
To those whose spirits hearken) as one

Who, in a dream of night, *would* fly,
But *cannot* from a danger nigh.

What tho' the moon—the white moon—
Shed all the splendor of her noon,
Her smile is chilly, and *her* beam,
In that time of dreariness, will seem
(So like you gather in your breath)
A portrait taken after death.
And boyhood is a summer sun
Whose waning is the dreariest one—
For all we live to know is known
And all we seek to keep hath flown—
Let life, then, as the day-flower, fall
With the noon-day beauty—which is all.

I reach'd my home—my home no more—
    For all had flown who made it so.
I pass'd from out its mossy door,
    And, tho' my tread was soft and low,
A voice came from the threshold stone
Of one whom I had earlier known—
    Oh, I defy thee, Hell, to show
    On beds of fire that burn below,
    An humbler heart—a deeper woe.

Father, I firmly do believe—
    I *know*—for Death who comes for me
        From regions of the blest afar,
Where there is nothing to deceive,
        Hath left his iron gate ajar,

And rays of truth you cannot see
Are flashing thro' Eternity——
I do believe that Eblis hath
A snare in every human path—
Else how, when in the holy grove
I wandered of the idol, Love,
Who daily scents his snowy wings
With incense of burnt offerings
From the most unpolluted things,
Whose pleasant bowers are yet so riven
Above with trellis'd rays from Heaven
No mote may shun—no tiniest fly—
The light'ning of his eagle eye—
How was it that Ambition crept,
   Unseen, amid the revels there,
Till growing bold, he laughed and leapt
   In the tangles of Love's very hair?

Ulalume

The skies they were ashen and sober;
    The leaves they were crisped and sere—
    The leaves they were withering and sere;
It was night in the lonesome October
    Of my most immemorial year;
It was hard by the dim lake of Auber,
    In the misty mid region of Weir—
It was down by the dank tarn of Auber,
    In the ghoul-haunted woodland of Weir.

Here once, through an alley Titanic,
    Of cypress, I roamed with my Soul—
    Of cypress, with Psyche, my Soul.
These were days when my heart was volcanic
    As the scoriac rivers that roll—
    As the lavas that restlessly roll
Their sulphurous currents down Yaanek
    In the ultimate climes of the pole—
That groan as they roll down Mount Yaanek
    In the realms of the boreal pole.

Our talk had been serious and sober,
    But our thoughts they were palsied and sere—
    Our memories were treacherous and sere,—
For we knew not the month was October,
    And we marked not the night of the year
    (Ah, night of all nights in the year!)—
We noted not the dim lake of Auber
    (Though once we had journey down here)—
Remembered not the dank tarn of Auber,
    Nor the ghoul-haunted woodland of Weir.

And now, as the night was senescent
    And star-dials pointed to morn—
    As the star-dials hinted of morn—
At the end of our path a liquescent
    And nebulous lustre was born,
Out of which a miraculous crescent
    Arose with a duplicate horn—
Astarte's bediamonded crescent
    Distinct with its duplicate horn.
And I said: "She is warmer than Dian:
    She rolls through an ether of sighs—
    She revels in a region of sighs:

She has seen that the tears are not dry on
    These cheeks, where the worm never dies,
And has come past the stars of the Lion
    To point us the path to the skies—
    To the Lethean peace of the skies—
Come up, in despite of the Lion,
    To shine on us with her bright eyes—
Come up through the lair of the Lion,
    With love in her luminous eyes."

But Psyche, uplifting her finger,
    Said: "Sadly this star I mistrust—
    Her pallor I strangely mistrust:—
Oh, hasten!—oh, let us not linger!
    Oh, fly!—let us fly!—for we must."
In terror she spoke, letting sink her
    Wings until they trailed in the dust—

In agony sobbed, letting sink her
        Plumes till they trailed in the dust—
        Till they sorrowfully trailed in the dust.

I replied: "This is nothing but dreaming:
        Let us on by this tremulous light!
        Let us bathe in this crystalline light!
Its Sybilic splendor is beaming
        With Hope and in Beauty to-night!—
        See!—it flickers up the sky through the night!
Ah, we safely may trust to its gleaming,
        And be sure it will lead us aright—
We safely may trust to a gleaming,
        That cannot but guide us aright,
        Since it flickers up to Heaven through the night."

Thus I pacified Psyche and kissed her,
        And tempted her out of her gloom—.
        And conquered her scruples and gloom;
And we passed to the end of the vista,
        But were stopped by the door of a tomb—
        By the door of a legended tomb;
And I said: "What is written, sweet sister,
        On the door of this legended tomb?"
        She replied: "Ulalume—Ulalume—
        'Tis the vault of thy lost Ulalume!"

Then my heart it grew ashen and sober
        As the leaves that were crisped and sere—
        As the leaves that were withering and sere,—
And I cried: "It was surely October

On *this* very night of last year
That I journeyed—I journeyed down here—
That I brought a dread burden down here—
On this night of all nights in the year,
Ah, what demon has tempted me here?
Well I know, now, this dim lake of Auber—
This misty mid region of Weir—
Well I know, now, this dank tarn of Auber,
This ghoul-haunted woodland of Weir."

A Valentine

For her this rhyme is penned, whose luminous eyes,
    Brightly expressive as the twins of Lœda,
Shall find her own sweet name, that, nestling lies
    Upon the page, enwrapped from every reader.
Search narrowly the lines!—they hold a treasure
    Divine—a talisman—an amulet
That must be worn *at heart*. Search well the measure—
    The words—the syllables! Do not forget
The trivialest point, or you may lose your labor!
    And yet there is in this no Gordian knot
Which one might not undo without a sabre,
    If one could merely comprehend the plot.
Enwritten upon the leaf where now are peering
    Eyes' scintillating soul, there lie *perdus*
Three eloquent words oft uttered in the hearing
    Of poets, by poets—as the name is a poet's too.
Its letters, although naturally lying
    Like the knight Pinto—Mendez Ferdinando—
Still form a synonym for Truth.—Cease trying!
    You will not read the riddle, though you do the best you
    can do.

[To translate the address, read the first letter of the first line in connection with the second letter of the second line, the third letter of the third line, the fourth of the fourth, and so on to the end. The name will thus appear.]

The Valley of Unrest

Once it smiled a silent dell
Where the people did not dwell:
They had gone unto the wars,
Trusting to the mild-eyed stars,
Nightly from their azure towers,
To keep watch above the flowers,
In the midst of which all day
The red sunlight lazily lay.
Now each visitor shall confess
The sad valley's restlessness.
Nothing there is motionless—
Nothing save the airs that brood
Over the magic solitude.
Ah, by no wind are stirred those trees
That palpitate like the chill seas
Around the misty Hebrides!
Ah, by no wind those clouds are driven
That rustle through the unquiet Heaven
Uneasily, from morn till even,
Over the violets there that lie
In myriad types of the human eye—
Over the lilies there that wave
And weep above a nameless grave!
They wave:—from out their fragrant tops
Eternal dews come down in drops.
They weep:—from off their delicate stems
Perennial tears descend in gems.

"In Youth I have Known One"

How often we forget all time, when lone
Admiring Nature's universal throne;
Her woods—her wilds—her mountains—the intense
Reply of Hers to Our intelligence!

I

In youth I have known one with whom the Earth
    In secret communing held—as he with it,
In daylight, and in beauty, from his birth:
    Whose fervid, flickering torch of life was lit
From the sun and stars, whence he had drawn forth
    A passionate light such for his spirit was fit—
And yet that spirit knew—not in the hour
Of its own fervor—what had o'er it power.

II

Perhaps it may be that my mind is wrought
    To a fever[1] by the moonbeam that hangs o'er,
But I will half believe that wild light fraught
    With more of sovereignty than ancient lore
Hath ever told—or is it of a thought
    The unembodied essence, and no more
That with a quickening spell doth o'er us pass
As dew of the night-time, o'er the summer grass?

[1]Query "fervor"?—ED.

III

Doth o'er us pass, when, as th' expanding eye
   To the loved object—so the tear to the lid
Will start, which lately slept in apathy?
     And yet it need not be—(that object) hid
From us in life—but common—which doth lie
   Each hour before us—but then only bid
With a strange sound, as of a harp-string broken
T'awake us—'Tis a symbol and a token—

IV

Of what in other worlds shall be—and given
   In beauty by our God, to those alone
Who otherwise would fall from life and Heaven
   Drawn by their heart's passion, and that tone,
That high tone of the spirit which hath striven
    Though not with Faith—with godliness—whose throne
With desperate energy 't hath beaten down;
Wearing its own deep feeling as a crown.

To Zante

Fair isle, that from the fairest of all flowers
    Thy gentlest of all gentle names dost take!
How many memories of what radiant hours
    At sight of thee and thine at once awake!
How many scenes of what departed bliss!
    How many thoughts of what entombed hopes!
How many visions of a maiden that is
    No more—no more upon thy verdant slopes!
No more! alas, that magical sad sound
    Transforming all! Thy charms shall please *no more!*
Thy memory *no more!* Accursed ground
    Henceforth I hold thy flower-enamelled shore,
O hyacinthine isle! O purple Zante!
    "Isola d'oro! Fior di Levante!"

The Rationale of Verse

THE WORD "VERSE" is here used not in its strict or primitive sense, but as the term most convenient for expressing generally and without pedantry all that is involved in the consideration of rhythm, rhyme, metre, and versification.

There is, perhaps, no topic in polite literature which has been more pertinaciously discussed, and there is certainly not one about which so much inaccuracy, confusion, misconception, misrepresentation, mystification, and downright ignorance on all sides, can be fairly said to exist. Were the topic really difficult, or did it lie, even, in the cloud-land of metaphysics, where the doubt-vapors may be made to assume any and every shape at the will or at the fancy of the gazer, we should have less reason to wonder at all this contradiction and perplexity; but in fact the subject is exceedingly simple; one tenth of it, possibly, may be called ethical; nine tenths, however, appertain to mathematics; and the whole is included within the limits of the commonest common-sense.

"But, if this is the case, how," it will be asked, "can so much misunderstanding have arisen? Is it conceivable that a thousand profound scholars, investigating so very simple a matter for centuries, have not been able to place it in the fullest light, at least, of which it is susceptible?" These queries, I confess, are not easily answered:—at all events, a satisfactory reply to them might cost more trouble, than would, if properly considered, the whole *vexata quæstio* to which they have reference. Nevertheless, there is little difficulty or danger in suggesting that the "thousand profound scholars" *may* have failed, first, because they were scholars, secondly, because they were profound, and thirdly, because they were a thousand—the impotency of the scholarship and profundity having been thus multiplied a thousand-fold. I am serious in these suggestions; for, first again, there is something in "scholarship" which seduces us into blind worship of Bacon's Idol of the Theatre—into irrational deference to antiquity; secondly, the proper "profundity" is rarely profound—it is the nature of truth in general, as of some ores in particular, to be richest when most superficial; thirdly, the clearest subject may be overclouded by mere superabundance of talk. In chemistry, the best way of separating two bodies is to add a third; in speculation, fact often agrees with fact and argument with argument, until an additional well-meaning fact or argument sets every thing by the ears. In one case out of a hundred a point is excessively discussed because it is obscure; in the ninety-nine remaining it is obscure because excessively discussed. When a topic is thus circumstanced, the readiest mode of investigating it is to forget that any previous investigation has been attempted.

But, in fact, while much has been written on the Greek and Latin rhythms, and even on the Hebrew, little effort has been made at examining that of any of the modern tongues. As regards the English, comparatively nothing has been done. It may be said, indeed, that we are without a treatise on our own verse. In our ordinary grammars and in our works on rhetoric or prosody in general, may be found occasional chapters, it is true, which have the heading "Versification," but these are, in all instances, exceedingly meagre. They pretend to no analysis; they propose nothing like system; they make no attempt at even rule; every thing depends upon "authority." They are confined, in fact, to mere exemplification of the supposed varieties of English feet and English lines;—although in no work with which I am acquainted are these feet correctly given or these lines detailed in any thing like their full extent. Yet what has been mentioned is all—if we except the occasional introduction of some pedagogue-ism, such as this, borrowed from the Greek Prosodies: "When a syllable is wanting, the verse is said to be catalectic; when the measure is exact, the line is acatalectic; when there is a redundant syllable it forms hypermeter." Now whether a line be termed catalectic or acatalectic is, perhaps, a point of no vital importance; it is even possible that the student may be able to decide, promptly, when the *a* should be employed and when omitted, yet be incognizant, at the same time, of *all* that is worth knowing in regard to the structure of verse.

A leading defect in each of our treatises (if treatises they can be called), is the confining the subject to mere *Versification,* while *Verse* in general, with the understanding given to the term in the heading of this paper, is the real question at issue. Nor am I aware of even one of our grammars which so much as properly defines the word versification itself. "Versification," says a work now before me, of which the accuracy is far more than usual—the "English Grammar" of Goold Brown,—"Versification is the art of arranging words into lines of correspondent length, so as to produce harmony by the regular alternation of syllables differing in quantity." The commencement of this definition might apply, indeed, to the *art* of versification, but not versification itself. Versification is not the art of arranging, etc., but the actual arranging—a distinction too obvious to need comment. The error here is identical with one which has been too long permitted to disgrace the initial page of every one of our school grammars. I allude to the definitions of English grammar itself. "English grammar," it is said, "is the art of speaking and writing the English language correctly." This phraseology, or something essentially similar, is employed, I believe, by Bacon, Miller, Fisk, Greenleaf, Ingersoll, Kirkland, Cooper, Flint, Pue, Comly, and many others. These gentlemen, it is presumed, adopted it without examination from Murray, who derived it from Lily (whose work was *"quam solam Regia Majestas in omnibus scholis docendam præcipit"*), and who appropriated it without acknowledgment, but with some unimportant modification, from the Latin Grammar of Leonicenus. It may be shown, however, that this definition, so complacently received, it not, and cannot be, a proper definition of English grammar. A definition is that which so describes its object as to distinguish it from all others; it is no definition of any one thing if its terms are applicable to any one other. But if it be asked: "What is the design—the end—the aim of English grammar?" our obvious answer is: "The art of speaking and writing the English language correctly,"—that is to say, we must use the precise words employed as the definition of English grammar itself. But the object to be attained by any means is, assuredly, not the means. English grammar and the end contemplated by English grammar are two matters sufficiently distinct; nor can the one be more reasonably regarded as the other than a fishing-hook as a fish. The definition, therefore, which is applicable in the latter instance, *cannot,* in the former, be true. Grammar in general is the analysis of language; English grammar of the English.

But to return to Versification as defined in our extract above. "It is the art," says the extract, "of arranging words into lines *of correspondent length.*" Not so; a correspondence in the length of lines is by no means essential. Pindaric odes are, surely, instances of versification, yet these compositions are noted for extreme diversity in the length of their lines.

The arrangement is, moreover, said to be for the purpose of producing "*harmony* by the regular alternation," etc. But *harmony* is not the sole aim— not even the principal one. In the construction of verse, *melody* should never be left out of view; yet this is a point which all our prosodies have most unaccountably forborne to touch. Reasoned rules on this topic should form a portion of all systems of rhythm.

"So as to produce harmony," says the definition, "by the *regular alternation,*" etc. A *regular* alternation, as described, forms no part of any principle of versification. The arrangement of spondees and dactyls, for example, in the Greek hexameter, is an arrangement which may be termed *at random.* At least it is arbitrary. Without interference with the line as a whole, a dactyl may be substituted for a spondee, or the converse, at any point other than the ultimate and penultimate feet, of which the former is always a spondee, the latter nearly always a dactyl. Here, it is clear, we have no "*regular* alternation of syllables differing in quantity."

"So as to produce harmony," proceeds the definition, "by the regular alternation of *syllables differing in quantity,*"—in other words, by the alternation of long and short syllables; for in rhythm all syllables are necessarily either short or long. But not only do I deny the necessity of any *regularity* in the succession of feet and, by consequence, of syllables, but dispute the essentiality of any *alternation,* regular or irregular, of syllables long and short. Our author, observe, is now engaged in a definition of versification in general, not of English versification in particular. But the Greek and Latin metres abound in the spondee and pyrrhic—the former consisting of two long syllables, the latter of two short; and there are innumerable instances of the immediate succession of many spondees and many pyrrhics.

Here is a passage from Silius Italicus:

> Fallis te mensas inter quod credis inermem
> Tot bellis quæsita viro, tot cædibus armat
> Majestas eterna ducem: si admoveris ora
> Cannas et Trebium ante oculos Trasymenaque busta,
> Et Pauli stare ingentem miraberis umbram.

Making the elisions demanded by the classic prosodies, we should scan these hexameters thus:

> Fāllīs | tē mēn | sās īn | tēr qūod | crēdĭs ĭn | ērmēm |
> Tōt bēl | līs qūæ | sītă vĭ | rō tōt | cædĭbŭs | ārmāt |
> Mājēs | tās ē | tērnă dŭ | cēm s'ād | mōvĕrĭs | ōrā |
> Cānnās | ēt Trĕbĭ' | ānt'ŏcŭ | lōs Trăsy | mēnăqŭe | būstā |
> Et Pāu | lī stā | r'īngēn | tēm mī | rābĕrĭs | ūmbrām |

It will be seen that, in the first and last of these lines, we have only two short syllables in thirteen, with an uninterrupted succession of no less than *nine* long syllables. But how are we to reconcile all this with a definition of versification which describes it as "the art of arranging words into lines of correspondent length so as to produce harmony by the *regular alternation of syllables differing in quantity*"?

It may be urged, however, that our prosodist's *intention* was to speak of the English metres alone, and that, by omitting all mention of the spondee and pyrrhic, he has virtually avowed their exclusion from our rhythms. A grammarian is never excusable on the ground of good intentions. We demand from him, if from any one, rigorous precision of style. But grant the design. Let us admit that our author, following the example of all authors on English Prosody, has, in defining versification at large, intended a definition merely of the English. All these prosodists, we will say, reject the spondee and pyrrhic. Still all admit the iambus, which consists of a short syllable followed by a long; the trochee, which is the converse of the iambus; the dactyl, formed of one long syllable followed by two short; and the anapæst—two short succeeded by a long. The spondee is improperly rejected, as I shall presently show. The pyrrhic is rightfully dismissed. Its existence in either ancient or modern rhythm is purely chimerical, and the insisting on so perplexing a nonentity as a foot of *two short* syllables, affords, perhaps, the best evidence of the gross irrationality and subservience to authority which characterize our Prosody. In the meantime the acknowledged dactyl and anapæst are enough to sustain my proposition about the "alternation," etc., without reference to feet which are assumed to exist in the Greek and Latin metres alone: for an anapæst and a dactyl may meet in the same line; when, of course, we shall have an uninterrupted succession of four short syllables. The meeting of these two feet, to be sure, is an accident not contemplated in the definition now discussed; for this definition, in demanding a "regular alternation of syllables differing in quantity," insists on a regular succession of similar *feet*. But here is an example:

Sīng tŏ mĕ | Isăbēlle.

This is the opening line of a little ballad now before me, which proceeds in the same rhythm—a peculiarly beautiful one. More than all this: English lines are often well composed, entirely, of a regular succession of syllables *all of the same quantity*—the first lines, for instance, of the following quatrain by Arthur C. Coxe:

March! march! march!
    Making sounds as they tread.
Ho! ho! how they step,
    Going down to the dead!

The line italicised is formed of three cæsuras. The cæsura, of which I have much to say hereafter, is rejected by the English Prosodies and grossly misrepresented in the classic. It is a perfect foot—the most important in all verse—and consists of a single *long* syllable; *but the length of this syllable varies.*

It has thus been made evident that there is *not one* point of the definition in question which does not involve an error. And for any thing more satisfactory or more intelligible we shall look in vain to any published treatise on the topic.

So general and so total a failure can be referred only to radical misconception. In fact the English Prosodists have blindly followed the pedants. These latter, like *les moutons de Panurge,* have been occupied in incessant tumbling into ditches, for the excellent reason that their leaders have so tumbled before. The Iliad, being taken as a starting-point, was made to stand in stead of Nature and common-sense. Upon this poem, in place of facts and deduction from fact, or from natural law, were built systems of feet, metres, rhythms, rules,—rules that contradict each other every five minutes, and for nearly all of which there may be found twice as many exceptions as examples. If any one has a fancy to be thoroughly confounded—to see how far the infatuation of what is termed "classical scholarship" can lead a book-worm in the manufacture of darkness out of sunshine, let him turn over, for a few moments, any of the German Greek prosodies. The only thing clearly made out in them is a very magnificent contempt for Leibnitz' principle of "a sufficient reason."

To divert attention from the real matter in hand by any farther reference to these works, is unnecessary, and would be weak. I cannot call to mind, at this moment, one essential particular of information that is to be gleaned from them; and I will drop them here with merely this one observation: that, employing from among the numerous *"ancient"* feet the spondee, the trochee, the iambus, the anapæst, the dactyl, and the cæsura alone, I will engage to scan *correctly* any of the Horatian rhythms, or any true rhythm that human ingenuity can conceive. And this excess of chimerical feet is, perhaps, the very least of the scholastic supererogations. *Ex uno disce omnia.* The fact is that *Quantity* is a point in whose investigation the lumber of mere learning may be dispensed with, if ever in any. Its appreciation is universal. It appertains to no region, nor race, nor era in especial. To melody and to harmony the Greeks hearkened with ears precisely similar to those which we employ for similar purposes at present; and I should not be condemned for heresy in asserting that a pendulum at Athens would have vibrated much after the same fashion as does a pendulum in the city of Penn.

Verse originates in the human enjoyment of equality, fitness. To this enjoyment, also, all the moods of verse—rhythm, metre, stanza, rhyme, alliteration, the *refrain,* and other analogous effects—are to be referred. As there are some readers who habitually confound rhythm and metre, it may be as well here to say that the former concerns the *character* of feet (that is, the arrangements of syllables) while the latter has to do with the *number* of these feet. Thus, by "a dactylic *rhythm*" we express a sequence of dactyls. By "a dactylic hexa*meter*" we imply a line or measure consisting of six of these dactyls.

To return to *equality.* Its idea embraces those of similarity, proportion, identity, repetition, and adaptation or fitness. It might not be very difficult to go even behind the idea of equality, and show both how and why it is that the human nature takes pleasure in it, but such an investigation would, for any purpose now in view, be supererogatory. It is sufficient that the *fact* is undeniable—the fact that man derives enjoyment from his perception of equality. Let us examine a crystal. We are at once interested by the equality between the sides and between the angles of one of its faces: the equality of the sides pleases us; that of the angles doubles the pleasure. On bringing to view a second face in all respects similar to the first, this pleasure seems to be squared; on bringing to view a third, it appears to be cubed, and so on. I have no doubt, indeed, that the delight experienced, if measurable, would be found to have exact mathematical relations such as I suggest; that is to say, as far as a certain point, beyond which there would be a decrease in similar relations.

The perception of pleasure in the equality of *sounds* is the principle of *Music*. Unpractised ears can appreciate only simple equalities, such as are found in ballad airs. While comparing one simple sound with another they are too much occupied to be capable of comparing the equality subsisting between these two simple sounds, taken conjointly, and two other similar simple sounds taken conjointly. Practised ears, on the other hand, appreciate both equalities at the same instant—although it is absurd to suppose that both are *heard* at the same instant. One is heard and appreciated from itself: the other is heard by the memory; and the instant glides into and is confounded with the secondary, appreciation. Highly cultivated musical taste in this manner enjoys not only these double equalities, all appreciated at once, but takes pleasurable cognizance, through memory, of equalities the members of which occur at intervals so great that the uncultivated taste loses them altogether. That this latter can properly estimate or decide on the merits of what is called scientific music, is of course impossible. But scientific music has no claim to intrinsic excellence—it is fit for scientific ears alone. In its excess it is the triumph of the *physique* over the *morale* of music. The sentiment is overwhelmed by the sense. On the whole, the advocates of a simpler melody and harmony have infinitely the best of the argument; although there has been very little of real argument on the subject.

In *verse,* which cannot be better designated than as an inferior or less capable Music, there is, happily, little chance for perplexity. Its rigidly simple character not even Science—not even Pedantry can greatly pervert.

The rudiment of verse may, possibly, be found in the *spondee.* The very germ of a thought seeking satisfaction in equality of sound, would result in the construction of words of two syllables, equally accented. In corroboration of this idea we find that spondees most abound in the most ancient tongues. The second step we can easily suppose to be the comparison, that is to say, the collocation, of two spondees—of two words composed each of a spondee. The third step would be the juxtaposition of three of these words. By this time the perception of monotone would induce farther consideration: and thus arises what Leigh Hunt so flounders in discussing under the title of "The *Principle* of Variety in Uniformity." Of course there is no principle in the case—nor in maintaining it. The "Uniformity" is the principle; the "Variety" is but the principle's natural safeguard from self-destruction by excess of self. "Uniformity," besides, is the very worst word that could have been chosen for the expression of the *general* idea at which it aims.

The perception of monotone having given rise to an attempt at its relief, the first thought in this new direction would be that of collating two or more words formed each of two syllables differently accented (that is to say, short and long) but having the same order in each word,—in other terms, of collating two or more iambuses, or two or more trochees. And here let me pause to assert that more pitiable nonsense has been written on the topic of *long* and *short* syllables than on any other subject under the sun. In general, a syllable is long or short, just as it is difficult or easy of enunciation. The *natural* long syllables are those encumbered—the *natural* short syllables are those *un*encumbered, with consonants; all the rest is mere artificiality and jargon. The Latin prosodies have a rule that "a vowel before two consonants is long." This rule is deduced from "authority"—that is, from the observation that vowels so circumstanced, in the ancient poems, are always in syllables long by the laws of scansion. The philosophy of the rule is untouched, and lies simply in the physical difficulty of giving voice to such syllables—of performing the lingual evolutions necessary for their utterance. Of course, it is not the *vowel* that is long (although the rule says so), but the syllable of which the vowel is a part. It will be seen that the length of a syllable, depending on the facility or difficulty of its enunciation, must have great variation in various syllables; but for the purposes of verse we suppose a long syllable equal to two short ones:—and the natural deviation from this relativeness we correct in perusal. The more closely our long syllables approach this relation with our short ones, the better, *ceteris paribus,* will be our verse: but if the relation does not exist of itself, we force it by emphasis, which can, of course, make any syllable as long as desired;— or, by an effort we can pronounce with unnatural brevity a syllable that is naturally too long. *Accented* syllables are of course always long—but, where *un*encumbered with consonants, must be classed among the *unnaturally* long. Mere custom has declared that we shall accent them—that is to say, dwell upon them; but no inevitable lingual difficulty forces us to do so. In line, every long syllable must of its own accord occupy in its utterance, or must be *made* to occupy, precisely the time demanded for two short ones. The only exception to this rule is found in the cæsura—of which more anon.

The success of the experiment with the trochees or iambuses (the one would have suggested the other) must have led to a trial of dactyls or anapæsts—natural dactyls or anapæsts—dactylic or anapæstic *words.* And now some degree of complexity has been attained. There is an appreciation, first, of the equality between the several dactyls, or anapæsts, and, secondly, of that between the long syllable and the two short conjointly. But here it may be said that step after step would have been taken, in continuation of this routine, until all the feet of the Greek prosodies became exhausted. Not so; these remaining feet have no existence except in the brains of the scholiasts. It is needless to imagine men inventing these things, and folly to explain how and why they invented them, until it shall be first shown that they are actually invented. All other "feet" than those which I have specified, are, if not impossible at first view, merely combinations of the specified; and, although this assertion is rigidly true, I will, to avoid misunderstanding, put it in a somewhat different shape. I will say, then, that at present I am aware of no *rhythm*—nor do I believe that any one can be constructed—which, in its last analysis, will not be found to consist altogether of the feet I have mentioned, either existing in their individual and obvious condition, or interwoven with each other in accordance with simple natural laws which I will endeavor to point out hereafter.

We have now gone so far as to suppose men constructing indefinite sequences of spondaic, iambic, trochaic, dactylic, or anapæstic words. In *extending* the sequences, they would be again arrested by the sense of monotone. A succession of spondees would *immediately* have displeased; one of iambuses or of trochees, on account of the variety included within the foot itself, would have taken longer to displease; one of dactyls or anapæsts, still longer; but even the last, if extended very far, must have become wearisome. The idea, first, of curtailing, and, secondly, of defining the length of, a sequence, would thus at once have arisen. Here then is the *line,* or verse proper.[1] The principle of equality being constantly at the bottom of the whole process, lines would naturally be made, in the first instance, equal in the number of their feet; in the second instance, there would be variation in the mere number: one line would be twice as long as another; then one would be some less obvious multiple of another; then still less obvious proportions would be adopted;—nevertheless there would be *proportion,* that is to say, a phase of equality, still.

Lines being once introduced, the necessity of distinctly defining these lines *to the ear* (as yet written verse does not exist), would lead to a scrutiny of their capabilities *at their terminations:*—and now would spring up the idea of

---

[1]Verse, from the Latin *vertere,* to turn, is so called on account of the turning or recommencement of the series of feet. Thus a verse, strictly speaking, is a line. In this sense, however, I have preferred using the latter word alone; employing the former in the general acceptation given it in the heading of this paper.

equality in sound between the final syllables—in other words, of *rhyme*. First, it would be used only in the iambic, anapæstic, and spondaic rhythms (granting that the latter had not been thrown aside, long since, on account of its tameness), because in these rhythms, the concluding syllable being long, could best sustain the necessary protraction of the voice. No great while could elapse, however, before the effect, found pleasant as well as useful, would be applied to the two remaining rhythms. But as the chief force of rhyme must lie in the accented syllable, the attempt to create rhyme at all in these two remaining rhythms, the trochaic and dactylic, would necessarily result in double and triple rhymes, such as *beauty* with *duty* (trochaic) and *beautiful* with *dutiful* (dactylic).

It must be observed, that in suggesting these processes, I assign them no date; nor do I even insist upon their order. Rhyme is supposed to be of modern origin, and were this proved, my positions remain untouched. I may say, however, in passing, that several instances of rhyme occur in the "Clouds" of Aristophanes, and that the Roman poets occasionally employ it. There is an effective species of ancient rhyming which has never descended to the moderns: that in which the ultimate and penultimate syllables rhyme with each other. For example:

Parturiunt montes et nascitur ridi*culus mus*.

And again:

Litoreis ingens inventa sub ilici*bus sus*.

The terminations of Hebrew verse (as far as understood) show no signs of rhyme; but what thinking person can doubt that it did actually exist? That men have so obstinately and blindly insisted, *in general,* even up to the present day, in confining rhyme to the *ends* of lines, when its effect is even better applicable elsewhere, intimates, in my opinion, the sense of some *necessity* in the connection of the end with the rhyme,—hints that the origin of rhyme lay in a necessity which connected it with the end,—shows

that neither mere accident nor mere fancy gave rise to the connection,—
points, in a word, at the very necessity which I have suggested (that of some
mode of defining lines *to the ear*) as the true origin of rhyme. Admit this,
and we throw the origin far back in the night of Time—beyond the origin
of written verse.

But, to resume. The amount of complexity I have now supposed to be
attained is very considerable. Various systems of equalization are appreciated
at once (or nearly so) in their respective values and in the value of each
system with reference to all the others. As our present *ultimatum* of
complexity, we have arrived at triple-rhymed, natural-dactylic lines, existing
proportionally as well as equally with regard to other triple-rhymed,
natural-dactylic lines. For example:

> Virginal Lilian, rigidly, humblily, dutiful;
> > Saintlily, lowlily,
> > Thrillingly, holily
> Beautiful!

Here we appreciate, first, the absolute equality between the long syllable of
each dactyl and the two short conjointly; secondly, the absolute equality
between each dactyl and any other dactyl—in other words, among all the
dactyls; thirdly, the absolute equality between the two middle lines; fourthly,
the absolute equality between the first line and the three others taken
conjointly; fifthly, the absolute equality between the last two syllables of the
respective words "dutiful" and "beautiful"; sixthly, the absolute equality
between the two last syllables of the respective words "lowlily" and
"holily"; seventhly, the proximate equality between the first syllable of
"dutiful" and the first syllable of "beautiful"; eighthly, the proximate
equality between the first syllable of "lowlily" and that of "holily"; ninthly,
the proportional equality (that of five to one) between the first line and
each of its members, the dactyls; tenthly, the proportional equality (that of
two to one) between each of the middle lines and its members, the dactyls;

eleventhly, the proportional equality between the first line and each of the two middle—that of five to two; twelfthly, the proportional equality between the first line and the last—that of five to one; thirteenthly, the proportional equality between each of the middle lines and the last—that of two to one; lastly, the proportional equality, as concerns number, between all the lines, taken collectively and any individual line—that of four to one.

The consideration of this last equality would give birth immediately to the idea of *stanza*[2]—that is to say, the insulation of lines into equal or obviously proportional masses. In its primitive (which was also its best) form, the stanza would most probably have had absolute unity. In other words, the removal of any one of its lines would have rendered it imperfect; as in the case above, where, if the last line, for example, be taken away, there is left no rhyme to the "dutiful" of the first. Modern stanza is excessively loose— and where so, ineffective, as a matter of course.

Now, although in the deliberate written statement which I have here given of these various systems of equalities, there seems to be an infinity of complexity—so much that it is hard to conceive the mind taking cognizance of them all in the brief period occupied by the perusal or recital of the stanza—yet the difficulty is in fact apparent only when we will it to become so. Any one fond of mental experiment may satisfy himself, by trial, that, in listening to the lines, he does actually (although with a seeming unconsciousness, on account of the rapid evolutions of sensation) recognize and instantaneously appreciate (more or less intensely as his ear is cultivated) each and all of the equalizations detailed. The pleasure received, or receivable, has very much such progressive increase, and in very nearly such mathematical relations, as those which I have suggested in the case of the crystal.

It will be observed that I speak of merely a proximate equality between the first syllable of "dutiful" and that of "beautiful"; and it may be asked why

---

[2]A stanza is often vulgarly, and with gross impropriety, called a *verse*.

we cannot imagine the earliest rhymes to have had absolute instead of proximate equality of sound. But absolute equality would have involved the use of identical words; and it is the duplicate sameness or monotony—that of sense as well as that of sound—which would have caused these rhymes to be rejected in the very first instance.

The narrowness of the limits within which verse composed of natural feet alone must necessarily have been confined, would have led, after a *very* brief interval, to the trial and immediate adoption of artificial feet—that is to say, of feet *not* constituted each of a single word, but two or even three words; or of parts of words. These feet would be intermingled with natural ones. For example:

    ă brēath | căn māke | thĕm ās | ă brēath | hăs māde.

This is an iambic line in which each iambus is formed of two words. Again:

    Thĕ ūn | ĭmā | gĭnā | blĕ mīght | ŏf Jōve.

This is an iambic line in which the first foot is formed of a word and a part of a word; the second and third, of parts taken from the body or interior of a word; the fourth, of a part and a whole; the fifth, of two complete words. There are no *natural* feet in either lines. Again:

    Cān ĭt bĕ | fāncĭĕd thăt | Dēĭty | ēvĕr vĭn | dīctĭvely
    Māde ĭn hĭs | īmăge ă | mānnĭkĭn | mērely tŏ | māddĕn ĭt?

These are two dactylic lines in which we find natural feet ("Deity," "mannikin"), feet composed of two words ("fancied that," "image a," "merely to," "madden it"), feet composed of three words ("can it be," "made in his"), a foot composed of a part of a word ("dictively"), and a foot composed of a word and a part of a word ("ever vin").

And now, in our supposititious progress, we have gone so far as to exhaust all the *essentialities* of verse. What follows may, strictly speaking, be regarded as embellishment merely—but even in this embellishment, the rudimental sense of *equality* would have been the never-ceasing impulse. It would, for example, be simply in seeking farther administration to this sense that men would come, in time, to think of the *refrain,* or burden, where, at the closes of the several stanzas of a poem, one word or phrase is *repeated;* and of alliteration, in whose simplest form a consonant is *repeated* in the commencements of various words. This effect would be extended so as to embrace repetitions both of vowels and of consonants, in the bodies as well as in the beginnings of words; and, at a later period would be made to infringe on the province of rhyme, by the introduction of general similarity of sound between whole feet occurring in the body of a line:—all of which modifications I have exemplified in the line above,

Made in his image a *mannikin* merely to *madden it.*

Farther cultivation would improve also the *refrain* by relieving its monotone in slightly varying the phrase at each repetition, or (as I have attempted to do in "The Raven") in retaining the phrase and varying its application— although this latter point is not strictly a rhythmical effect *alone.* Finally, poets when fairly wearied with following precedent—following it the more closely the less they perceived it in company with Reason—would adventure so far as to indulge in positive rhyme at other points than the ends of lines. First, they would put it in the middle of the line; then at some point where the multiple would be less obvious; then, alarmed at their own audacity, they would undo all their work by cutting these lines in two. And here is the fruitful source of the infinity of "short metre," by which modern poetry, if not distinguished, is at least disgraced. It would require a high degree, indeed, both of cultivation and of courage, on the part of any versifier, to enable him to place his rhymes—and let them remain—at unquestionably their best position, that of unusual and *unanticipated* intervals.

On account of the stupidity of some people, or (if talent be a more respectable word), on account of their talent for misconception—I think it necessary to add here, first, that I believe the "processes" above detailed to be nearly if not accurately those which *did* occur in the gradual creation of what we now call verse; secondly, that, although I so believe, I yet urge neither the assumed fact nor my belief in it as a part of the true propositions of this paper; thirdly, that in regard to the aim of this paper, it is of no consequence whether these processes did occur either in the order I have assigned them, or at all; my design being simply, in presenting a general type of what such processes *might* have been and *must* have resembled, to help *them,* the "some people," to an easy understanding of what I have farther to say on the topic of Verse.

There is one point which, in my summary of the processes, I have purposely forborne to touch; because this point, being the most important of all, on account of the immensity of error usually involved in its consideration, would have led me into a series of detail inconsistent with the object of a summary.

Every reader of verse must have observed how seldom it happens that even any one line proceeds uniformly with a succession, such as I have supposed, of absolutely equal feet; that is to say, with a succession of iambuses only, or of trochees only, or of dactyls only, or of anapæsts only, or of spondees only. Even in the most musical lines we find the succession interrupted. The iambic pentameters of Pope, for example, will be found, on examination, frequently varied by trochees in the beginning, or by (what seem to be) anapæsts in the body, of the line.

Ŏh thoū whătē | vĕr tī | tlĕ plēase | thĭne ēar |
Dĕan Drā | pĭĕr Bīck | ĕrstäff | ŏr Gūl | ĭvēr |
Whēthĕr | thŏu choōse | Cĕrvān | tĕs' sē | rĭoŭs aīr |
Ŏr laūgh | ănd shāke | ĭn Rāb | ĕlăis' ēa | sy chāir. |

Were any one weak enough to refer to the prosodies for the solution of the difficulty here, he would find it *solved* as usual by a *rule,* stating the fact (or what it, the rule, supposes to be the fact), but without the slightest attempt at the *rationale*. "By a *synæresis* of the two short syllables," say the books, "an anapæst may sometimes be employed for an iambus, or a dactyl for a trochee. ★ ★ ★ In the beginning of a line a trochee is often used for an iambus."

Blending is the plain English for *synæresis*—but there should be *no* blending; neither is an anapæst *ever* employed for an iambus, or a dactyl for a trochee. These feet differ in time; and *no* feet so differing can ever be legitimately used in the same line. An anapæst is equal to four short syllables—an iambus only to three. Dactyls and trochees hold the same relation. The principle of *equality,* in verse, admits, it is true, of variation at certain points, for the relief of monotone, as I have already shown, but the point of *time* is that point which, being the rudimental one, must never be tampered with at all.

To explain:—In farther efforts for the relief of monotone than those to which I have alluded in the summary, men soon came to see that there was no absolute necessity for adhering to the precise number of syllables, provided the time required for the whole foot was preserved inviolate. They saw, for instance, that in such a line as

ŏr laūgh | ănd shāke | ĭn Rāb | ĕlăis' ēa | sy chāir, |

the equalization of the three syllables *elais' ea* with the two syllables composing any of the other feet, could be readily effected by pronouncing the two syllables *elais'* in double quick time. By pronouncing each of the syllables *e* and *lais'* twice as rapidly as the syllable *sy,* or the syllable *in,* or any other syllable, they could bring the two of them, taken together, to the length, that is to say, to the time, of any one short syllable. This consideration enabled them to effect the agreeable variation of three syllables in place of the uniform two. And variation was the object— variation to the ear. What sense is there, then, in supposing this object rendered null by the *blending* of the two syllables so as to render them, in absolute effect, one? Of course, there must be *no* blending. Each syllable must be pronounced as distinctly as possible (or the variation is lost), but with twice the rapidity in which the ordinary syllable is enunciated. That the syllables *elais' ea* do not compose an *anapæst* is evident, and the signs (ăăā) of their accentuation are erroneous. The foot might be written thus (ăăā), the inverted crescents expressing double quick time; and might be called a bastard iambus.

Here is a trochaic line:

   Sēe thĕ dēlĭcăte | fŏotĕd | rēin-deĕr. |

The prosodies—that is to say, the most considerate of them—would here decide that *"delicate"* is a dactyl used in place of a trochee, and would refer to what they call their "rule," for justification. Others, varying the stupidity, would insist upon a Procrustean adjustment thus (del-cate)—an adjustment recommended to all such words as *silvery, murmuring,* etc., which, it is said, should be not only pronounced, but written *silv'ry, murm'ring,* and so on, whenever they find themselves in trochaic predicament. I have only to say that "delicate," when circumstanced as above, is neither a dactyl nor a dactyl's equivalent; that I would suggest for it this (ăăā) accentuation; that I think it as well to call it a bastard trochee; and that all words, at all events, should be written and pronounced *in full,* and as nearly as possible as nature intended them.

About eleven years ago, there appeared in the *American Monthly Magazine* (then edited, I believe, by Messrs. Hoffman and Benjamin) a review of Mr. Willis' Poems; the critic putting forth his strength or his weakness, in an endeavor to show that the poet was either absurdly affected, or grossly ignorant of the laws of verse; the accusation being based altogether on the fact that Mr. W. made occasional use of this very word "delicate," and other similar words, in "the Heroic measure, which every one knew consisted of feet of two syllables." Mr. W. has often, for example, such lines as

That binds him to a woman's *delicate* love—
In the gay sunshine, *reverent* in the storm—
With its *invisible* fingers my loose hair.

Here, of course, the feet *licate love, verent in,* and *sible fin,* are bastard iambuses; are *not* anapæsts; and are *not* improperly used. Their employment, on the contrary, by Mr. Willis, is but one of the innumerable instances he has given of keen sensibility in all those matters of taste which may be classed under the general head of *fanciful embellishment.*

It is also about eleven years ago, if I am not mistaken, since Mr. Horne (of England), the author of "Orion," one of the noblest epics in any language, thought it necessary to preface his "Chaucer Modernized" by a very long and evidently a very elaborate essay, of which the greater portion was occupied in a discussion of the seemingly anomalous foot of which we have been speaking. Mr. Horne upholds Chaucer in its frequent use; maintains his superiority, *on account* of his so frequently using it, over all English versifiers; and, indignantly repelling the common idea of those who make verse on their fingers, that the superfluous syllable is a roughness and an error, very chivalrously makes battle for it as "a grace." That a grace it *is,* there can be no doubt; and what I complain of is, that the author of the most happily versified long poem in existence, should have been under the necessity of discussing this grace merely *as* a grace, through forty or fifty vague pages, solely because of his inability to show *how* and *why* it is a grace—by which showing the question would have been settled in an instant.

About the trochee used for an iambus, as we see in the beginning of the line,

> Whēthĕr thou choose Cervantes' serious air,

there is little that need be said. It brings me to the general proposition that in all rhythms, the prevalent or distinctive feet may be varied at will, and nearly at random, by the *occasional* introduction of equivalent feet—that is to say, feet the sum of whose syllabic times is equal to the sum of the syllabic times of the distinctive feet. Thus the trochee *whēthĕr,* is equal in the sum of the times of its syllables, to the iambus, *thoŭ chōose,* in the sum of the times of *its* syllables; each foot being, in time, equal to three short syllables. Good versifiers, who happen to be, also, good poets, contrive to relieve the monotone of a series of feet, by the use of equivalent feet only at rare intervals, and at such points of their subject as seem in accordance with the *startling* character of the variation. Nothing of this care is seen in the line quoted above—although Pope has some fine instances of the duplicate effect. Where vehemence is to be strongly expressed, I am not sure that we should be wrong in venturing on *two consecutive* equivalent feet—although I cannot say that I have ever known the adventure made, except in the following passage, which occurs in "Al Aaraaf," a boyish poem, written by myself when a boy. I am referring to the sudden and rapid advent of a star:

> Dim was its little disk, and angel eyes
> Alone could see the phantom in the skies,
> Whĕn first thĕ phāntŏm's cōurse wăs foūnd tŏ bē
> *Hēadlŏng hīthĕr*ward o'er the starry sea.

In the "general proposition" above, I speak of the *occasional* introduction of equivalent feet. It sometimes happens that unskilful versifiers, without knowing what they do, or why they do it, introduce so many "variations" as to exceed in number the "distinctive" feet; when the ear becomes at once balked by the *bouleversement* of the rhythm. Too many trochees, for example, inserted in an iambic rhythm, would convert the latter to a trochaic. I may note here, that, in all cases, the rhythm designed should be commenced and continued, *without* variation, until the ear has had full time to comprehend what *is* the rhythm. In violation of a rule so obviously founded in common-sense, many even of our best poets, do not scruple to begin an iambic rhythm with a trochee, or the converse; or a dactylic with an anapæst, or the converse; and so on.

A somewhat less objectionable error, although still a decided one, is that of commencing a rhythm, not with a different equivalent foot, but with a "bastard" foot of the rhythm intended. For example:

Māny ă | thōught wĭll | cōme tŏ | mēmŏry. |

Here *many a* is what I have explained to be a bastard trochee, and to be understood should be accented with inverted crescents. It is objectionable solely on account of its position as the *opening* foot of a trochaic rhythm. *Memory,* similarly accented, is also a bastard trochee, but *un*objectionable, although by no means demanded.

The farther illustration of this point will enable me to take an important step.

One of the finest poets, Mr. Christopher Pease Cranch, begins a very beautiful poem thus:

Many are the thoughts that come to me
    In my lonely musing;
And they drift so strange and swift
    There's no time for choosing
Which to follow; for to leave
    Any, seems a losing.

"A losing" to Mr. Cranch, of course—but this *en passant.* It will be seen here that the intention is trochaic, although we do *not* see this intention by the opening foot, as we should do—or even by the opening line. Reading the whole stanza, however, we perceive the trochaic rhythm as the general design, and so, after some reflection, we divide the first line thus:

Many are the | thōughts thăt | cōme tŏ | mē. |

Thus scanned, the line will seem musical. It *is*—highly so. And it is because there is no end to instances of just such lines of apparently incomprehensible music, that Coleridge thought proper to invent his nonsensical *system* of what he calls "scanning by accents"—as if "scanning by accents" were any thing more than a phrase. Wherever "Christabel" is really *not rough,* it can be as readily scanned by the true *laws* (not the supposititious *rules*) of verse as can the simplest pentameter of Pope and where it *is* rough (*passim*), these same laws will enable any one of common-sense to show *why* it is rough, and to point out, instantaneously, the remedy for the roughness.

A reads and re-reads a certain line, and pronounces it false in rhythm— unmusical. *B,* however, reads it *to A,* and *A* is at once struck with the perfection of the rhythm, and wonders at his dulness in not "catching" it before. Henceforward he admits the line to be musical. *B,* triumphant, asserts that, to be sure, the line is musical—for it is the work of Coleridge,—and that it is *A* who is *not;* the fault being in *A's* false reading. Now here *A* is right and *B* wrong. *That* rhythm is erroneous (at some point or other more or less obvious) which *any* ordinary reader *can,* without design, read improperly. It is the business of the poet so to construct his line that the intention *must* be caught *at once.* Even when these men have precisely the same understanding of a sentence, they differ, and often widely, in their modes of enunciating it. Any one who has taken the trouble to examine the topic of emphasis (by which I here mean not *accent* of particular syllables, but the dwelling on entire words), must have seen that men emphasize in the most singularly arbitrary manner. There are certain large classes of people, for example, who persist in emphasizing their monosyllables. Little uniformity of emphasis prevails; because the thing itself—the idea, emphasis—is referable to no natural, at least to no well-comprehended and therefore uniform, law. Beyond a very narrow and vague limit, the whole matter is conventionality. And if we differ in emphasis even when we agree in comprehension, how much more so in the former when in the latter too! Apart, however, from the consideration of natural disagreement, is it not clear that, by tripping here and mouthing there, any sequence of words may be twisted into any species of rhythm? But are we thence to deduce that all sequences of words are rhythmical in a rational understanding of the term?—for this is the deduction, precisely to which the *reductio ad absurdum* will, in the end, bring all the propositions of Coleridge. Out of a hundred readers of "Christabel," fifty will be able to make nothing of its rhythm, while forty-nine of the remaining fifty will, with some ado, fancy they comprehend it, after the fourth or fifth perusal. The one out of the whole hundred who shall both comprehend and admire it at first sight must be an unaccountably clever person—and I am by far too modest to assume, for a moment, that that very clever person is myself.

In illustration of what is here advanced I cannot do better than quote a poem:

> Pease porridge hot—pease porridge cold—
> Pease porridge in the pot—nine days old.

Now those of my readers who have never *heard* this poem pronounced according to the nursery conventionality, will find its rhythm as obscure as an explanatory note; while those who *have* heard it, will divide it thus, declare it musical, and wonder how there can be any doubt about it.

> Pease | porridge | hot | pease | porridge | cold |
> Pease | porridge | in the | pot | nine | days | old. |

The chief thing in the way of this species of rhythm, is the necessity which it imposes upon the poet of travelling in constant company with his compositions, so as to be ready, at a moment's notice, to avail himself of a well understood poetical license—that of reading aloud one's own doggerel.

In Mr. Cranch's line,

> Many are the | thoughts that | come to | me, |

the general error of which I speak is, of course, very partially exemplified, and the purpose for which, chiefly, I cite it, lies yet farther on in our topic.

The two divisions (*thoughts that*) and (*come to*) are ordinary trochees. Of the last division (*me*) we will talk hereafter. The first division (many are the) would be thus accented by the Greek prosodies (mānȳ ăre thĕ) and would be called by them αστρολογος. The Latin books would style the foot *Pæon Primus,* and both Greek and Latin would swear that it was composed of a trochee and what they term a pyrrhic—that is to say, a foot of two *short* syllables—a thing that *cannot be,* as I shall presently show.

But now, there is an obvious difficulty. The *astrologos,* according to the prosodies' own showing, is equal to *five* short syllables, and the trochee to *three*—yet, in the line quoted, these two feet are equal. They occupy *precisely* the same time. In fact, the whole music of the line depends upon their being *made* to occupy the same time. The prosodies then, have demonstrated what all mathematicians have stupidly failed in demonstrating—that three and five are one and the same thing.

After what I have already said, however, about the bastard trochee and the bastard iambus, no one can have any trouble in understanding that *many are the* is of similar character. It is merely a bolder variation than usual from the routine of trochees, and introduces to the bastard trochee one additional syllable. But this syllable is not *short.* That is, it is not short in the sense of *"short"* as applied to the final syllable of the ordinary trochee, where the word means merely *the half of long.*

In this case (that of the additional syllable), "short," if used at all, must be used in the sense of *the sixth of long.* And all the three final syllables can be called *short* only with the same understanding of the term. The three together are equal only to the one short syllable (whose place they supply) of the ordinary trochee. It follows that there is no sense in thus (˘) accenting these syllables. We must devise for them some new character which shall denote the sixth of long. Let it be (c)—the crescent placed with the curve to the left. The whole foot (mānȳ ăre thĕ) might be called a *quick trochee.*

We come now to the final division (*me*) of Mr. Cranch's line. It is clear that this foot, short as it appears, is fully equal in time to each of the preceding. It is in fact the cæsura—the foot which, in the beginning of this paper, I called the most important in all verse. Its chief office is that of pause or termination; and here—at the end of a line—its use is easy, because there is no danger of misapprehending its value. We pause on it, by a seeming necessity, just as long as it has taken us to pronounce the preceding feet, whether iambuses, trochees, dactyls, or anapæsts. It is thus a *variable foot,* and, with some care, may be well introduced into the body of a line, as in a little poem of great beauty by Mrs. Welby:

.....
I have | a lit | tle step | son | of on | ly three | years old. |

Here we dwell on the cæsura, *son,* just as long as it requires us to pronounce either of the preceding or succeeding iambuses. Its value, therefore, in this line, is that of three short syllables. In the following dactylic line its value is that of four short syllables.

....
Pale as a | lily was | Emily | Gray. |

I have accentuated the cæsura with a dotted line (......) by way of expressing this variability of value.

I observed just now that there could be no such foot as one of two short syllables. What we start from in the very beginning of all idea on the topic of verse, is quantity, *length.* Thus when we enunciate an independent syllable it is long, as a matter of course. If we enunciate two, dwelling on both equally, we express equality in the enumeration, or length, and have a right to call them two long syllables. If we dwell on one more than the other, we have also a right to call one short, because it is short in relation to the other. But if we dwell on both equally and with a tripping voice, saying to ourselves here are two short syllables, the query might well be asked of us—"in relation to what are they short?" Shortness is but the negation of length. To say, then, that two syllables, placed independently of any other syllable, are short, is merely to say that they have no positive length, or enunciation—in other words that they are no syllables—that they do not exist at all. And if, persisting, we add any thing about their equality, we are merely floundering in the idea of an identical equation, where, x being equal to x, nothing is shown to be equal to zero. In a word, we can form no conception of a pyrrhic as of an independent foot. It is a mere chimera bred in the mad fancy of a pedant.

From what I have said about the equalization of the several feet of a *line,* it must not be deduced that any *necessity* for equality in time exists between the rhythm of *several* lines. A poem, or even a stanza, may begin with iambuses, in the first line, and proceed with anapæsts in the second, or even with the less accordant dactyls, as in the opening of quite a pretty specimen of verse by Miss Mary A. S. Aldrich.

> The wa | ter li | ly sleeps | in pride | ....
>   Dōwn ĭn thĕ | dēpths ŏf thĕ | āzūre | lake. |

Here *azure* is a spondee, equivalent to a dactyl; *lake,* a cæsura.

I shall now best proceed in quoting the initial lines of Byron's "Bride of Abydos":

> Know ye the land where the cypress and myrtle
>   Are emblems of deeds that are done in their clime—
> Where the rage of the vulture, the love of the turtle
>   Now melt into softness, now madden to crime?
> Know ye the land of the cedar and vine,
> Where the flowers ever blossom, the beams ever shine,
> And the light wings of Zephyr, oppressed with perfume,
> Wax faint o'er the gardens of Gul in their bloom?
> Where the citron and olive are fairest of fruit
> And the voice of the nightingale never is mute—
> Where the virgins are soft as the roses they twine,

And all save the spirit of man is divine?
'Tis the land of the East—'tis the clime of the Sun—
Can he smile on such deeds as his children have done?
Oh, wild as the accents of lovers' farewell
Are the hearts that they bear and the tales that they tell!

Now the flow of these lines (as times go) is very sweet and musical. They have been often admired, and justly—as times go,—that is to say, it is a rare thing to find better versification of its kind. And where verse is pleasant to the ear, it is silly to find fault with it because it refuses to be scanned. Yet I have heard men, professing to be scholars, who made no scruple of abusing these lines of Byron's on the ground that they were musical in spite of *all law*. Other gentlemen, *not* scholars, abused "all law" for the same reason; and it occurred neither to the one party nor to the other that the law about which they were disputing might possibly be no law at all—an ass of a law in the skin of a lion.

The grammars said something about dactylic lines, and it was easily seen that *these* lines were at least meant for dactylic. The first one was, therefore, thus divided:

Knōw yĕ thĕ | lānd whĕre thĕ | cyprĕss ănd | myrtlĕ |

The concluding foot was a mystery; but the prosodies said something about the dactylic "measure" calling now and then for a double rhyme; and the court of inquiry were content to rest in the double rhyme, without exactly perceiving what a double rhyme had to do with the question of an irregular foot. Quitting the first line, the second was thus scanned:

Arē ĕmblĕms | ōf dĕeds thăt | āre dŏne ĭn | thēir clĩme. |

It was immediately seen, however, that *this* would not do,—it was at war with the whole emphasis of the reading. It could not be supposed that Byron, or any one in his senses, intended to place stress upon such monosyllables as "are," "of," and "their," nor could "their clime," collated with "to crime," in the corresponding line below, be fairly twisted into any thing like a "double rhyme," so as to bring every thing within the category of the grammars. But farther these grammars spoke not. The inquirers, therefore, in spite of their sense of harmony in the lines, when considered without reference to scansion, fell back upon the idea that the "Are" was a blunder,—an excess for which the poet should be sent to Coventry,—and, striking it out, they scanned the remainder of the line as follows:

—— ēmblĕms ŏf | dēeds thăt ăre | dōne ĭn thĕir | clīme. |

This answered pretty well; but the grammars admitted no such foot as a foot of one syllable; and besides the rhythm was dactylic. In despair, the books are well searched, however, and at last the investigators are gratified by a full solution of the riddle in the profound "Observation" quoted in the beginning of this article:—"When a syllable is wanting, the verse is said to be catalectic; when the measure is exact, the line is acatalectic; when there is a redundant syllable it forms hypermeter." This is enough. The anomalous line is pronounced to be catalectic at the head and to form hypermeter at the tail,—and so on. and so on; it being soon discovered that nearly all the remaining lines are in a similar predicament, and that what flows so smoothly to the ear, although so roughly to the eye, is, after all, a mere jumble of catalecticism, acatalecticism, and hypermeter—not to say worse.

Now, had this court of inquiry been in possession of even the shadow of the *philosophy* of Verse, they would have had no trouble in reconciling this oil and water of the eye and ear, by merely scanning the passage without reference to lines, and, continuously, thus:

Know ye the | land where the | cypress and | myrtle Are | emblems of | deeds that are | done in their | clime Where the | rage of the | vulture the | love of the | turtle Now | melt into | softness now | madden to | *crime* | Know ye the | land of the | cedar and | vine Where the | flowers ever | blossom the | beams ever | shine Where the | light wings of | Zephyr op | pressed by

per | *fume Wax* | faint o'er the | gardens of | Gul in their | bloom
Where the | citron and | olive are | fairest of | fruit And the |
voice of the | nightingale | never is | mute Where the | virgins are
| soft as the | roses they | *twine And* | all save the | spirit of | man
is di | vine 'Tis the | land of the | East 'tis the | clime of the | Sun
Can he | smile on such | deeds as his | children have | *done Oh* |
wild as the | accents of | lovers' fare | well Are the | hearts that
they | bear and the | tales that they | *tell.*

Here "crime" and "tell" (italicized) are cæsuras, each having the value of a
dactyl, four short syllables; while *"fume Wax," "twine And,"* and *"done
Oh,"* are spondees, which, of course, being composed of two long syllables,
are also equal to four short, and are the dactyl's natural equivalent. The
nicety of Byron's ear has led him into a succession of feet which, with two
trivial exceptions as regards melody, are absolutely accurate—a very rare
occurrence this in dactylic or anapæstic rhythms. The exceptions are found
in the spondee *"twine And,"* and the dactyl, *"smile on such."* Both feet are
false in point of melody. In *"twine And,"* to make out the rhythm, we must
force *"And"* into a length which it will not naturally bear. We are called on
to sacrifice either the proper length of the syllable as demanded by its
position as a member of a spondee, or the customary accentuation of the
word in conversation. There is no hesitation, and should be none. We at
once give up the sound for the sense; and the rhythm is imperfect. In this
instance it is *very* slightly so;—not one person in ten thousand could, by
ear, detect the inaccuracy. But the *perfection* of Verse, as regards melody,
consists in its *never* demanding any such sacrifice as is here demanded. The
rhythmical must agree, *thoroughly,* with the reading flow. This perfection has
in no instance been attained—but is unquestionably attainable. *"Smile on
such,"* the dactyl, is incorrect, because *"such,"* from the character of the
two consonants *ch,* cannot *easily* be enunciated in the ordinary time of a
short syllable, which its position declares that it is. Almost every reader will
be able to appreciate the slight difficulty here; and yet the error is by no

means so important as that of the *"And,"* in the spondee. By dexterity we *may* pronounce *"such"* in the true time; but the attempt to remedy the rhythmical deficiency of the *"And"* by drawing it out, merely aggravates the offence against natural enunciation, by directing attention to the offence.

My main object, however, in quoting these lines, is to show that, in spite of the prosodies, the length of a line is entirely an arbitrary matter. We might divide the commencement of Byron's poem thus:

Know ye the | land where the |

or thus:

Know ye the | land where the | cypress and |

or thus:

Know ye the | land where the | cypress and | myrtle are |

or thus:

Know ye the | land where the | cypress and | myrtle are | emblems of |

In short, we may give it any division we please, and the lines will be good—provided we have at least *two* feet in a line. As in mathematics two units are required to form number, so rhythm (from the Greek αριϑμος, number) demands for its formation at least two feet. Beyond doubt, we often see such lines as

Know ye the—
Land where the—

lines of one foot; and our prosodies admit such; but with impropriety: for common-sense would dictate that every so obvious division of a poem as is made by a line, should include within itself all that is necessary for its own comprehension; but in a line of one foot we can have no appreciation of *rhythm,* which depends upon the equality between *two* or more pulsations. The false lines, consisting sometimes of a single cæsura, which are seen in mock Pindaric odes, are of course "rhythmical" only in connection with some other line; and it is this want of independent rhythm which adapts them to the purposes of burlesque alone. Their effect is that of incongruity (the principle of mirth), for they include the blankness of prose amid the harmony of verse.

My second object in quoting Byron's lines, was that of showing how absurd it often is to cite a single line from amid the body of a poem, for the purpose of instancing the perfection or imperfection of the line's rhythm. Were we to see by itself

> Know ye the land where the cypress and myrtle,

we might justly condemn it as defective in the final foot, which is equal to only three, instead of being equal to four, short syllables.

In the foot *"flowers ever"* we shall find a further exemplification of the principle of the bastard iambus, bastard trochee, and quick trochee, as I have been at some pains in describing these feet above. All the Prosodies on English Verse would insist upon making an elision in *"flowers,"* thus *"flow'rs,"* but this is nonsense. In the quick trochee *"mānỹ ăre thĕ"* occurring in Mr. Cranch's *trochaic* line, we had to equalize the time of the three syllables *"any, are, the"* to that of the one *short* syllable whose position they usurp. Accordingly each of these syllables is equal to the third of a short syllable—that is to say, the *sixth of a long.* But in Byron's *dactylic* rhythm, we have to equalize the time of the three syllables *"ers, ev, er"* to that of the one *long* syllable whose position they usurp, or (which is the same thing) of the *two short.* Therefore, the value of each of the syllables *"ers, ev,* and *er"* is the *third of a long.* We enunciate them with only half the rapidity we employ in enunciating the three final syllables of the quick trochee—which latter is a rare foot. The *"flowers ever,"* on the contrary, is as common in the dactylic rhythm as is the *bastard* trochee in the trochaic, or the bastard iambus in the iambic. We may as well accent it with the curve of the crescent to the right, and call it a *bastard dactyl.* A *bastard anapæst,* whose nature I now need be at no trouble in explaining, will of course occur, now and then, in an anapæstic rhythm.

In order to avoid any chance of that confusion which is apt to be introduced in an essay of this kind by too sudden and radical an alteration of the conventionalities to which the reader has been accustomed, I have thought it right to suggest for the accent marks of the bastard trochee, bastard iambus, etc., etc., certain characters which, in merely varying the direction of the ordinary short accent (˘), should imply, what is the fact, that the feet themselves are not *new* feet, in any proper sense, but simply modifications of the feet, respectively, from which they derive their names. Thus a bastard iambus is, in its essentiality,—that is to say, in its time,—an iambus. The variation lies only in the *distribution* of this time. The time, for example, occupied by the one short (or *half of long*) syllable, in the ordinary iambus, is, in the bastard, spread equally over two syllables, which are accordingly the *fourth of long.*

But this fact—the fact of the essentiality, or whole time, of the foot being unchanged—is now so fully before the reader that I may venture to propose, finally, an accentuation which shall answer the real purpose—that is to say, what should be the real purpose of all accentuation—the purpose of expressing to the eye the exact relative value of every syllable employed in Verse.

I have already shown that enunciation, or *length,* is the point from which we start. In other words, we begin with a *long syllable.* This, then, is our unit; and there will be no need of accenting it at all. An unaccented syllable, in a system of accentuation, is to be regarded always as a long syllable. Thus a spondee would be without accent. In an iambus, the first syllable being "short," or the *half* of long, should be accented with a small 2, placed *beneath* the syllable; the last syllable, being long, should be unaccented: the whole would be thus (control). In a trochee, these accents would be merely conversed, thus (manly). In a dactyl, each of the two final syllables, being the half of long, should, also, be accented with a small 2 beneath the syllable; and, the first syllable left unaccented, the whole would be thus (happiness). In an anapæst we should converse the dactyl, thus (in the land). In the bastard dactyl, each of the three concluding syllables being the *third* of long, should be accented with a small 3 beneath the syllable, and the whole foot would stand thus (flowers ever). In the bastard anapæst we should converse the bastard dactyl, thus (in the rebound). In the bastard iambus, each of the two initial syllables, being the *fourth* of long, should be accented below with a small 4; the whole foot would be thus (in the rain).

In the bastard trochee we should converse the bastard iambus, thus (many a). In the quick trochee, each of the three concluding syllables, being the *sixth* of long, should be accented below with a small 6; the whole foot would be thus (many are the). The quick iambus is not yet created, and most probably never will be, for it will be excessively useless, awkward, and liable to misconception,—as I have already shown that even the quick trochee is,—but, should it appear, we must accent it by conversing the quick trochee. The cæsura, being variable in length, but always *longer than* "*long,*" should be accented *above,* with a number expressing the length or value of the distinctive foot of the rhythm in which it occurs. Thus a cæsura, occurring in a spondaic rhythm, would be accented with a small 2 above the syllable, or, rather, foot. Occurring in a dactylic or anapæstic rhythm, we also accent it with the 2, above the foot. Occurring in an iambic rhythm, however, it must be accented, above, with $1\frac{1}{2}$, for this is the relative value of the iambus. Occurring in the trochaic rhythm, we give it, of course, the same accentuation. For the complex 1 ½, however, it would be advisable to substitute the simpler expression, ³/₂, which amounts to the same thing.

In this system of accentuation Mr. Cranch's lines, quoted above, would thus be written:

$$^3/_2$$
Many are the | thoughts that | come to | me
  6 6 6   2   2

  In my | lonely | musing, |
     2   2

$$^3/_2$$
And they | drift so | strange and | swift
   2   2   2

  There's no | time for | choosing |
     2   2   2

$$^3/_2$$
Which to | follow, | for to | leave
   2   2   2

  Any | seems a | losing. |
   2   2   2

In the ordinary system the accentuation would be thus:

Mānў arĕ thĕ | thōughts thăt | cōme tŏ | mē
  In my | lōnely | mūsĭng, |
And thĕў | drīft sō | strānge ănd | swīft |
  Thēre's nŏ | tīme fŏr | choōsĭng |
Whīch tŏ | fōllŏw, | fōr tŏ | lēave
  Any | sēems ă | lōsĭng. |

It must be observed here that I do not grant this to be the "ordinary" *scansion*. On the contrary, I never yet met the man who had the faintest comprehension of the true scanning of these lines, or of such as these. But granting this to be the mode in which our prosodies would divide the feet, they would accentuate the syllables as just above.

Now, let any reasonable person compare the two modes. The first advantage seen in my mode is that of simplicity—of time, labor, and ink saved. Counting the fractions as *two* accents, even, there will be found only *twenty-six* accents to the stanza. In the common accentuation there are *forty-one*. But admit that all this is a trifle, which it is *not,* and let us proceed to points of importance. Does the common accentuation express the truth in particular, in general, or in any regard? Is it consistent with itself? Does it convey either to the ignorant or to the scholar a just conception of the rhythm of the lines? Each of these questions must be answered in the negative. The crescents, being precisely similar, must be understood as expressing, all of them, one and the same thing; and so all prosodies have always understood them and wished them to be understood. They express, indeed, "short"; but this word has all kinds of meanings. It serves to represent (the reader is left to guess *when*) sometimes the half, sometimes the third, sometimes the fourth, sometimes the sixth of "long"; while "long" itself, in the books, is left undefined and undescribed. On the other hand, the horizontal accent, it may be said, expresses sufficiently well and unvaryingly the syllables which are meant to be long. It does nothing of the kind. This horizontal accent is placed over the cæsura (wherever, as in the Latin Prosodies, the cæsura is recognized) as well as over the ordinary long syllable, and implies any thing and every thing, just as the crescent. But grant that it does express the ordinary long syllables (leaving the cæsura out of question), have I not given the identical expression by not employing any expression at all? In a word, while the prosodies, with a certain number of accents express *precisely nothing whatever,* I, with scarcely half the number, have expressed every thing which, in a system of accentuation, demands expression. In glancing at my mode in the lines of Mr. Cranch it will be seen that it conveys not only the exact relation of the syllables and feet, among themselves, in those particular lines, but their precise value in relation to any other existing or conceivable feet or syllables in any existing or conceivable system of rhythm.

The object of what we call *scansion* is the distinct marking of the rhythmical flow. Scansion with accents or perpendicular lines between the feet—that is to say, scansion *by* the voice only—is scansion *to* the ear only; and all very good in its way. The written scansion addresses the ear through the eye. In either case the object is the distinct marking of the rhythmical, musical, or reading flow. There *can* be no other object, and there is none. Of course, then, the scansion and the reading flow should go hand-in-hand. The former must agree with the latter. The former represents and expresses the latter; and is good or bad as it truly or falsely represents and expresses it. If by the written scansion of a line we are not enabled to perceive any rhythm or music in the line, then either the line is unrhythmical or the scansion false. Apply all this to the English lines which we have quoted, at various points, in the course of this article. It will be found that the scansion exactly conveys the rhythm, and thus thoroughly fulfils the only purpose for which scansion is required.

But let the scansion *of the schools* be applied to the Greek and Latin verse, and what result do we find?—that the verse is one thing and the scansion quite another. The ancient verse, *read* aloud, is in general musical, and occasionally *very* musical. *Scanned* by the prosodial rules we can, for the most part, make nothing of it whatever. In the case of the English verse, the more emphatically we dwell on the divisions between the feet, the more distinct is our perception of the kind of rhythm intended. In the case of the Greek and Latin, the more we dwell the *less* distinct is this perception. To make this clear by an example:

> Mæcenas, atavis edite regibus,
> O, et præsidium et dulce decus meum,
> Sunt quos curriculo pulverem Olympicum
> Collegisse juvat, metaque fervidis
> Evitata rotis, palmaque nobilis
> Terrarum dominos evehit ad Deos.

Now in *reading* these lines, there is scarcely one person in a thousand who, if even ignorant of Latin, will not immediately feel and appreciate their flow—their music. A prosodist, however, informs the public that the *scansion* runs thus:

Mæce | nas ata | vis | edite | regibus |
O et | præsidi' | et | dulce de | cus meum |
Sunt quos | curricu | lo | pulver' O | lympicum |
Colle | gisse ju | vat | metaque | fervidis |
Evi | tata ro | tis | palmaque | nobilis |
Terra | rum domi | nos | evehit | ad Deos. |

Now I do not deny that we get a *certain sort* of music from the lines if we read them according to this scansion, but I wish to call attention to the fact that this scansion, and the certain sort of music which grows out of it, are entirely at war not only with the reading flow which any ordinary person would naturally give the lines, but with the reading flow universally given them, and never denied them, by even the most obstinate and stolid of scholars.

And now these questions are forced upon us: "Why exists this discrepancy between the modern verse with its scansion, and the ancient verse with its scansion?"—"Why, in the former case, are there agreement and representation, while in the latter there is neither the one nor the other?" or, to come to the point,—"How are we to reconcile the ancient verse with the scholastic scansion of it?" This absolutely necessary conciliation— shall we bring it about by supposing the scholastic scansion wrong because the ancient verse is right, or by maintaining that the ancient verse is wrong because the scholastic scansion is not to be gainsaid?

Were we to adopt the latter mode of arranging the difficulty, we might, in some measure, at least simplify the expression of the arrangement by putting it thus: Because the pedants have no eyes, therefore the old poets had no ears.

"But," say the gentlemen without the eyes, "the scholastic scansion, although certainly not handed down to us in form from the old poets themselves (the gentlemen without the ears), is nevertheless deduced from certain facts which are supplied us by careful observation of the old poems.

And let us illustrate this strong position by an example from an American poet—who must be a poet of some eminence, or he will not answer the purpose. Let us take Mr. Alfred B. Street. I remember these two lines of his:

> His sinuous path, by blazes, wound
> Among trunks grouped in myriads round.

With the *sense* of these lines I have nothing to do. When a poet is in a "fine frenzy," he may as well imagine a large forest as a small one; and "by blazes" is *not* intended for an oath. My concern is with the rhythm, which is iambic.

Now let us suppose that, a thousand years hence, when the "American language" is dead, a learned prosodist should be deducing, from "careful observation" of our best poets, a system of scansion for our poetry. And let us suppose that this prosodist had so little dependence in the generality and immutability of the laws of Nature, as to assume in the outset, that, because we lived a thousand years before his time, and made use of steam-engines instead of mesmeric balloons, we must therefore have had a *very* singular fashion of mouthing our vowels, and altogether of hudsonizing our verse. And let us suppose that with these and other fundamental propositions carefully put away in his brain, he should arrive at the line,—

> Among | trunks grouped | in my | riads round.

Finding it an obviously iambic rhythm, he would divide it as above; and observing that "trunks" made the first member of an iambus, he would call it short, as Mr. Street intended it to be. Now farther, if instead of admitting the possibility that Mr. Street (who by that time would be called Street simply, just as we say Homer)—that Mr. Street might have been in the habit of writing carelessly, as the poets of the prosodist's own era did, and as all poets will do (on account of being geniuses),—instead of admitting this, suppose the learned scholar should make a "rule" and put it in a book, to the effect that, in the American verse, the vowel *u, when found imbedded among nine consonants,* was *short,* what, under such circumstances, would the sensible people of the scholar's day have a right not only to think but to say of that scholar?—why, that he was "a fool—by blazes!"

I have put an extreme case, but it strikes at the root of the error. The "rules" are grounded in "authority"; and this "authority"—can any one tell us what it means? or can any one suggest any thing that it may *not* mean? Is it not clear that the "scholar" above referred to, might as readily have deduced from authority a totally false system as a partially true one? To deduce from authority a consistent prosody of the ancient metres would indeed have been within the limits of the barest possibility; and the task has *not* been accomplished, for the reason that it demands a species of ratiocination altogether out of keeping with the brain of a bookworm. A rigid scrutiny will show that the very few "rules" which have not as many exceptions as examples, are those which have, by accident, their true bases not in authority, but in the omniprevalent laws of syllabification; such, for example, as the rule which declares a vowel before two consonants to be long.

In a word, the gross confusion and antagonism of the scholastic prosody, as well as its marked inapplicability to the reading flow of the rhythms it pretends to illustrate, are attributable, first, to the utter absence of natural principle as a guide in the investigations which have been undertaken by inadequate men; and secondly, to the neglect of the obvious consideration that the ancient poems, which have been the *criteria* throughout, were the work of men who must have written as loosely, and with as little definitive system, as ourselves.

Were Horace alive to-day, he would divide for us his first Ode thus, and "make great eyes" when assured by prosodists that he had no business to make any such division!

Mæcenas | atavis | edite | regibus |

2 2   2 2   2 2   2 2

O et præ | sidium et | dulce de | cus meum |

2 2   3 3   3   2 2   2 2

Sunt quos cur | riculo | pulverem O | lympicum |

2   2   2 2   3   3   3   2 2

Collegisse | juvat | metaque | fervidis |

3   3 3   2 2   2 2

Evitata | rotis | palmaque | nobilis |

3   3 3   2 2   2 2

Terrarum | dominos | evehit | ad Deos. |

2 2   2 2   2 2   2 2

Read by this scansion, the flow is preserved; and the more we dwell on the divisions, the more the intended rhythm becomes apparent. Moreover, the feet have all the same time; while, in the scholastic scansion, trochees—admitted trochees—are absurdly employed as equivalents to spondees and dactyls. The books declare, for instance, that *Colle,* which begins the fourth line, is a trochee, and seem to be gloriously unconscious that to put a trochee in opposition with a longer foot, is to violate the inviolable principle of all music, *time.*

It will be said, however, by "some people," that I have no business to make a dactyl out of such obviously long syllables as *sunt, quos, cur.* Certainly I have no business to do so. I *never* do so. And Horace should not have done so. But he did. Mr. Bryant and Mr. Longfellow do the same thing every day. And merely because these gentlemen, now and then, forget themselves in this way, it would be hard if some future prosodist should insist upon twisting the "Thanatopsis," or the "Spanish Student," into a jumble of trochees, spondees, and dactyls.

It may be said, also, by some other people, that in the word *decus,* I have succeeded no better than the books, in making the scansional agree with the reading flow; and that *decus* was not pronounced de*cus*. I reply, that there can be no doubt of the word having been pronounced, in this case, de*cus*. It must be observed, that the Latin inflection, or variation of a word in its terminating syllable, caused the Romans—*must* have caused them—to pay greater attention to the termination of a word than to its commencement, or than we do to the terminations of our words. The end of the Latin word established that relation of the word with other words which we establish by prepositions or auxiliary verbs. Therefore, it would seem infinitely less odd to them than it does to us, to dwell at any time, for any slight purpose, abnormally, on a terminating syllable. In verse, this license—scarcely a license—would be frequently admitted. These ideas unlock the secret of such lines as the

> Litoreis ingens inventa sub ilici*bus sus,*

and the

> Parturiunt montes et nascitur ridicu*lus mus,*

which I quoted, some time ago, while speaking of rhyme.

As regards the prosodial elisions, such as that of *rem* before *O,* in *pulverem Olympicum,* it is really difficult to understand how so dismally silly a notion could have entered the brain even of a pedant. Were it demanded of me why the books cut off one *vowel* before another, I might say: It is, perhaps, because the books think that, since a bad reader is so apt to slide the one vowel into the other at any rate, it is just as well to print them *ready-slided.* But in the case of the terminating *m,* which is the most readily pronounced of all consonants (as the infantile *mamma* will testify), and the most impossible to cheat the ear of by any system of sliding—in the case of the *m,* I should be driven to reply that, to the best of my belief, the prosodists did the thing, because they had a fancy for doing it, and wished to see how funny it would look after it was done. The thinking reader will perceive that, from the great facility with which *em* may be enunciated, it is admirably suited to form one of the rapid short syllables in the bastard dactyl (pulverem O); but because the books had no conception of a bastard dactyl, they knocked it on the head at once—by cutting off its tail!

Let me now give a specimen of the true scansion of another Horatian measure—embodying an instance of proper elision.

Integer | vitæ | scelerisque | purus |
   2 2   3 3   3

Non eget | Mauri | jaculis ne | que arcu |
  2 2   3 3 3

Nec vene | natis | gravida sa | gittis |
  2 2   3 3 3

        Fusce pha | retrâ.
          2   2

Here the regular recurrence of the bastard dactyl gives great animation to the rhythm. The *e* before the *a* in *que arcu,* is, almost of sheer necessity, cut off—that is to say, run into the *a* so as to preserve the spondee. But even this license it would have been better not to take.

Had I space, nothing would afford me greater pleasure than to proceed with the scansion of *all* the ancient rhythms, and to show how easily, by the help of common-sense, the intended music of each and all can be rendered instantaneously apparent. But I have already overstepped my limits, and must bring this paper to an end.

It will never do, however, to omit all mention of the heroic hexameter.

I began the "processes" by a suggestion of the spondee as the first step toward verse. But the innate monotony of the spondee has caused its disappearance, as the basis of rhythm, from all modern poetry. We *may* say, indeed, that the French heroic—the most wretchedly monotonous verse in existence—is, to all intents and purposes, spondaic. But it is not designedly spondaic—and if the French were ever to examine it at all, they would no doubt pronounce it iambic. It must be observed that the French language is

Collected Poems

strangely peculiar in this point—*that it is without accentuation, and consequently without verse.* The genius of the people, rather than the structure of the tongue, declares that their words are, for the most part, enunciated with a uniform dwelling on each syllable. For example, *we* say "syl*lab*fi*ca*tion." A Frenchman would say syl-la-bi-fi-ca-ti-on; dwelling on no one of the syllables with any noticeable particularity. Here again I put an extreme case, in order to be well understood; but the general fact is as I give it—that, comparatively, the French have *no* accentuation. And there can be nothing worth the name of verse without. Therefore, the French have no verse worth the name—which is the fact, put in sufficiently plain terms. Their iambic rhythm so superabounds in absolute spondees, as to warrant me in calling its basis spondaic; but French is the *only* modern tongue which has any rhythm with such basis; and even in the French, it is, as I have said, unintentional.

Admitting, however, the validity of my suggestion, that the spondee was the first approach to verse, we should expect to find, first, natural spondees (words each forming just a spondee) most abundant in the most ancient languages; and, secondly, we should expect to find spondees forming the basis of the most ancient rhythms. These expectations are in both cases confirmed.

Of the Greek hexameter, the intentional basis is spondaic. The dactyls are the *variation* of the theme. It will be observed that there is no absolute certainty about *their* points of interposition. The penultimate foot, it is true, is usually a dactyl; but not uniformly so; while the ultimate, on which the ear *lingers,* is always a spondee. Even that the penultimate is usually a dactyl may be clearly referred to the necessity of winding up with the *distinctive* spondee. In corroboration of this idea, again, we should look to find the penultimate spondee most usual in the most ancient verse; and, accordingly, we find it more frequent in the Greek than in the Latin hexameter.

But besides all this, spondees are not only more prevalent in the heroic hexameter than dactyls, but occur to such an extent as is even unpleasant to modern ears, on account of monotony. What the modern chiefly appreciates and admires in the Greek hexameter, is the *melody of the abundant vowel sounds*. The Latin hexameters *really* please very few moderns— although so many pretend to fall into ecstasies about them. In the hexameters quoted, several pages ago, from Silius Italicus, the preponderance of the spondee is strikingly manifest. Besides the natural spondees of the Greek and Latin, numerous artificial ones arise in the verse of these tongues on account of the tendency which inflection has to throw full accentuation on terminal syllables; and the preponderance of the spondee is farther insured by the comparative infrequency of the small prepositions which *we* have to serve us *instead* of case, and also the absence of the diminutive auxiliary verbs with which *we* have to eke out the expression of our primary ones. These are the monosyllables whose abundance serve to stamp the poetic genius of a language as tripping or dactylic.

Now, paying no attention to these facts, Sir Philip Sidney, Professor Longfellow, and innumerable other persons more or less modern, have busied themselves in constructing what they suppose to be "English hexameters on the model of the Greek." The only difficulty was that (even leaving out of question the melodious masses of vowels) these gentlemen never could get their English hexameters to *sound* Greek. Did they *look* Greek?—that should have been the query; and the reply might have led to a solution of the riddle. In placing a copy of ancient hexameters side by side with a copy (in similar type) of such hexameters as Professor Longfellow, or Professor Felton, or the Frogpondian Professors collectively, are in the shameful practice of composing "on the model of the Greek," it will be seen that the latter (hexameters, not professors) are about one third longer *to the eye,* on an average, than the former. The more abundant dactyls make the difference. And it is the greater number of spondees in the Greek than in the English—in the ancient than in the modern tongue—which has caused it to fall out that while these eminent scholars were groping about in the dark for a Greek hexameter, which is a spondaic rhythm varied now and then by dactyls, they merely stumbled, to the lasting scandal of scholarship, over something which, on account of its long-leggedness, we may as well term a Feltonian hexameter, and which is a dactylic rhythm, interrupted, rarely, by artificial spondees which are no spondees at all, and which are curiously thrown in by the heels at all kinds of improper and impertinent points.

Here is a specimen of the Longfellownian hexameter.

> Also the | church with | in was a | dorned for | this was the |
> season
> In which the | young their | parents' | hope and the | loved ones of
> | Heaven |
> Should at the | foot of the | altar re | new the | vows of their |
> baptism |
> Therefore each | nook and | corner was | swept and | cleaned and
> the | dust was |
> Blown from the | walls and | ceiling and | from the | oil-painted |
> benches |

Mr. Longfellow is a man of imagination—but *can* he imagine that any individual, with a proper understanding of the danger of lock-jaw, would make the attempt of twisting his mouth into the shape necessary for the emission of such spondees as "par*ents,*" and "from the," or such dactyls as "cleaned and the," and "loved ones of"? "Baptism" is by no means a bad spondee—perhaps because it happens to be a dactyl;—of all the rest, however, I am dreadfully ashamed.

But these feet—dactyls and spondees, all together—should thus be put at once into their proper position:

Also, the church within was adorned; for this was the season in which the young, their parents' hope, and the loved ones of Heaven, should, at the foot of the altar, renew the vows of their baptism. Therefore each nook and corner was swept and cleaned; and the dust was blown from the walls and ceiling, and from the oil-painted benches.

There!—That is respectable prose; and it will incur no danger of ever getting its character ruined by anybody's mistaking it for verse.

But even when we let these modern hexameters go, as Greek, and merely hold them fast in their proper character of Longfellownian, or Feltonian, or Frogpondian, we must still condemn them as having been committed in a radical misconception of the philosophy of verse. The spondee, as I observed, is the *theme* of the Greek line. Most of the ancient hexameters *begin* with spondees, for the reason that the spondee *is* the theme; and the ear is filled with it as with a burden. Now the Feltonian dactylics have, in the same way, dactyls for the theme, and most of them begin with dactyls— which is all very proper if not very Greek,—but, unhappily, the one point at which they *are* very Greek is that point, precisely, at which they should be nothing but Feltonian. They always *close* with what is meant for a spondee. To be consistently silly, they should die off in a dactyl.

That a truly Greek hexameter *cannot,* however, be readily composed in English, is a proposition which I am by no means inclined to admit. I think I could manage the point myself. For example:

> Do tell! | when may we | hope to make | men of sense | out of the | Pundits |
> Born and brought | up with their | snouts deep | down in the | mud of the | Frog pond? |
> Why ask? | who ever | yet saw | money made | out of a | fat old |
> Jew, or | downright | upright | nutmegs | out of a | pine-knot? |

The proper spondee predominance is here preserved. Some of the dactyls are not so good as I could wish—but, upon the whole, the rhythm is very decent—to say nothing of its excellent sense.

The Poetic Principle

IN SPEAKING of the Poetic Principle, I have no design to be either thorough or profound. While discussing, very much at random, the essentiality of what we call Poetry, my principal purpose will be to cite for consideration, some few of those minor English or American poems which best suit my own taste, or which, upon my own fancy, have left the most definite impression. By "minor poems" I mean, of course, poems of little length. And here, in the beginning permit me to say a few words in regard to a somewhat peculiar principle, which, whether rightfully or wrongfully, has always had its influence in my own critical estimate of the poem. I hold that a long poem does not exist. I maintain that the phrase, "a long poem," is simply a flat contradiction in terms.

I need scarcely observe that a poem deserves its title only inasmuch as it excites, by elevating the soul. The value of the poem is in the ratio of this elevating excitement. But all excitements are, through a psychal necessity, transient. That degree of excitement which would entitle a poem to be so called at all, cannot be sustained throughout a composition of any great length. After the lapse of half an hour, at the very utmost, it flags—fails— a revulsion ensues—and then the poem is, in effect, and in fact, no longer such.

There are, no doubt, many who have found difficulty in reconciling the critical dictum that the "Paradise Lost" is to be devoutly admired throughout, with the absolute impossibility of maintaining for it, during perusal, the amount of enthusiasm which that critical dictum would demand. This great work, in fact, is to be regarded as poetical, only when, losing sight of that vital requisite in all works of Art, Unity, we view it merely as a series of minor poems. If, to preserve its Unity—its totality of effect or impression—we read it (as would be necessary) at a single sitting, the result is but a constant alternation of excitement and depression. After a passage of what we feel to be true poetry, there follows, inevitably, a passage of platitude which no critical prejudgment can force us to admire; but if upon completing the work, we read it again; omitting the first book—that is to say, commencing with the second—we shall be surprised at now finding that admirable which we before condemned—that damnable which we had previously so much admired. It follows from all this that the ultimate, aggregate, or absolute effect of even the best epic under the sun, is a nullity:— and this is precisely the fact.

In regard to the Iliad, we have, if not positive proof, at least very good reason, for believing it intended as a series of lyrics; but, granting the epic intention, I can say only that the work is based in an imperfect sense of Art. The modern epic is, of the supposititious ancient model, but an inconsiderate and blindfold imitation. But the day of these artistic anomalies is over. If, at any time, any very long poem *were* popular in reality—which I doubt—it is at least clear that no very long poem will ever be popular again.

That the extent of a poetical work, is *ceteris paribus,* the measure of its merit, seems undoubtedly, when we thus state it, a proposition sufficiently absurd—yet we are indebted for it to the quarterly Reviews. Surely there can be nothing in mere *size*, abstractly considered there can be nothing in mere *bulk*, so far as a volume is concerned, which has so continuously elicited admiration from these saturnine pamphlets! A mountain, to be sure, by the mere sentiment of physical magnitude which it conveys, *does* impress us with a sense of the sublime—but no man is impressed after *this* fashion by the material grandeur of even "The Columbiad." Even the Quarterlies have not instructed us to be so impressed by it. *As yet,* they have not *insisted* on our estimating Lamartine by the cubic foot, or Pollock by the pound—but what else are we to *infer* from their continual prating about "sustained effort"? If, by "sustained effort," any little gentleman has accomplished an epic, let us frankly commend him for the effort—if this indeed be a thing commendable,—but let us forbear praising the epic on the effort's account. It is to be hoped that common-sense, in the time to come, will prefer deciding upon a work of Art, rather by the impression it makes—by the effect it produces—than by the time it took to impress the effect, or by the amount of "sustained effort" which had been found necessary in effecting the impression. The fact is, that perseverance is one thing and genius quite another—nor can all the Quarterlies in Christendom confound them. By-and-by, this proposition, with many which I have been just urging, will be received as self-evident. In the meantime, by being generally condemned as falsities, they will not be essentially damaged as truths.

On the other hand, it is clear that a poem may be improperly brief. Undue brevity degenerates into mere epigrammatism. A *very* short poem, while now and then producing a brilliant or vivid, never produces a profound or enduring, effect. There must be the steady pressing down of the stamp upon the wax. De Béranger has wrought innumerable things, pungent and spirit-stirring; but, in general, they have been too imponderous to stamp themselves deeply into the public opinion; and thus, as so many feathers of fancy, have been blown aloft only to be whistled down the wind.

A remarkable instance of the effect of undue brevity in depressing a poem—in keeping it out of the popular view—is afforded by the following exquisite little Serenade:

I arise from dreams of thee
  In the first sweet sleep of night,
When the winds are breathing low,
  And the stars are shining bright.
I arise from dreams of thee,
  And a spirit in my feet

Has led me—who knows how?—
    To thy chamber-window, sweet!

The wandering airs they faint
    On the dark, the silent stream—
The champak odors fail
    Like sweet thoughts in a dream;
The nightingale's complaint,
    It dies upon her heart,
As I must die on thine,
    Oh, beloved as thou art!

Oh, lift me from the grass!
    I die, I faint, I fail!
Let thy love in kisses rain
    On my lips and eyelids pale.
My cheek is cold and white, alas!
    My heart beats loud and fast;
Oh, press it close to thine again,
    Where it will break at last!

Very few, perhaps, are familiar with these lines—yet no less a poet than
Shelley is their author. Their warm, yet delicate and ethereal imagination
will be appreciated by all—but by none so thoroughly as by him who has
himself arisen from sweet dreams of one beloved, to bathe in the aromatic
air of a southern midsummer night.

One of the finest poems by Willis—the very best, in my opinion, which he
has ever written—has, no doubt, through this same defect of undue brevity,
been kept back from its proper position, not less in the critical than in the
popular view.

    The shadows lay along Broadway,
        'Twas near the twilight-tide—

And slowly there a lady fair
  Was walking in her pride,
Alone walk'd she; but, viewlessly,
  Walk'd spirits at her side.

Peace charm'd the street beneath her feet,
  And Honor charm'd the air;
And all astir looked kind on her,
  And call'd her good as fair—
For all God ever gave to her,
  She kept with chary care.

She kept with care her beauties rare
  From lovers warm and true—
For her heart was cold to all but gold,
  And the rich came not to woo—
But honored well are charms to sell
  If priests the selling do.

Now walking there was one more fair—
  A slight girl, lily-pale;
And she had unseen company
  To make the spirit quail—
'Twixt Want and Scorn she walk'd forlorn,
  And nothing could avail.

No mercy now can clear her brow
  For this world's peace to pray;
For, as love's wild prayer dissolved in air,
  Her woman's heart gave way!—
But the sin forgiven by Christ in Heaven
  By man is cursed alway!

In this composition we find it difficult to recognize the Willis who has
written so many mere "verses of society." The lines are not only richly

ideal, but full of energy; while they breathe an earnestness—an evident sincerity of sentiment—for which we look in vain throughout all the other works of this author.

While the epic mania—while the idea that, to merit in poetry, prolixity is indispensable—has, for some years past, been gradually dying out of the public mind, by mere dint of its own absurdity, we find it succeeded by a heresy too palpably false to be long tolerated, but one which, in the brief period it has already endured, may be said to have accomplished more in the corruption of our Poetical Literature than all its other enemies combined. I allude to the heresy of *The Didactic*. It has been assumed, tacitly and avowedly, directly and indirectly, that the ultimate object of all Poetry is Truth. Every poem, it is said, should inculcate a moral; and by this moral is the poetical merit of the work to be adjudged. We Americans especially have patronized this happy idea; and we Bostonians, very especially, have developed it in full. We have taken it into our heads that to write a poem simply for the poem's sake, and to acknowledge such to have been our design, would be to confess ourselves radically wanting in the true Poetic dignity and force:—but the simple fact is, that, would we but permit ourselves to look into our own souls, we should immediately there discover that under the sun there neither exists nor *can* exist any work more thoroughly dignified—more supremely noble than this very poem—this poem *per se*—this poem which is a poem and nothing more—this poem written solely for the poem's sake.

With as deep a reverence for the True as ever inspired the bosom of man, I would, nevertheless, limit, in some measure, its modes of inculcation. I would limit to enforce them. I would not enfeeble them by dissipation. The demands of Truth are severe; she has no sympathy with the myrtles. All *that* which is so indispensable in Song, is precisely all *that* with which *she* has nothing whatever to do. It is but making her a flaunting paradox, to wreathe her in gems and flowers. In enforcing a truth, we need severity rather than efflorescence of language. We must be simple, precise, terse. We must be cool, calm, unimpassioned. In a word, we must be in that mood which, as nearly as possible, is the exact converse of the poetical. *He* must be blind indeed who does not perceive the radical and chasmal differences between the truthful and the poetical modes of inculcation. He must be theory-mad beyond redemption who, in spite of these differences, shall still persist in attempting to reconcile the obstinate oils and waters of Poetry and Truth.

Dividing the world of mind into its three most immediately obvious distinctions, we have the Pure Intellect, Taste, and the Moral Sense. I place Taste in the middle, because it is just this position which, in the mind, it occupies. It holds intimate relations with either extreme; but from the Moral Sense is separated by so faint a difference that Aristotle has not hesitated to place some of its operations among the virtues themselves. Nevertheless, we find the *offices* of the trio marked with a sufficient distinction. Just as the intellect concerns itself with Truth, so Taste informs us of the Beautiful, while the Moral Sense is regardful of Duty. Of this latter, while Conscience teaches the obligation, and Reason the expediency, Taste contents herself with displaying the charms:—waging war upon Vice solely on the ground of her deformity—her disproportion—her animosity to the fitting, to the appropriate, to the harmonious—in a word, to Beauty.

An immortal instinct, deep within the spirit of man, is thus, plainly, a sense of the Beautiful. This it is which administers to his delight in the manifold forms, and sounds, and odors, and sentiments amid which he exists. And just as the lily is repeated in the lake, or the eyes of Amaryllis in the mirror, so is the mere oral or written repetition of these forms, and sounds, and colors, and odors, and sentiments, a duplicate source of delight. But this mere repetition is not poetry. He who shall simply sing, with however glowing enthusiasm, or with however vivid a truth of description, of the sights, and sounds and odors, and colors, and sentiments, which greet *him* in common with all mankind—he, I say, has yet failed to prove his divine title. There is still a something in the distance which he has been unable to attain. We have still a thirst unquenchable, to allay which he has not shown us the crystal springs. This thirst belongs to the immortality of Man. It is at once a consequence and an indication of his perennial existence. It is the desire of the moth for the star. It is no mere appreciation of the Beauty before us—but a wild effort to reach the Beauty above. Inspired by an ecstatic prescience of the glories beyond the grave, we struggle, by multiform combinations among the things and thoughts of Time, to attain a portion of that Loveliness whose very elements, perhaps, appertain to eternity alone. And thus when by Poetry—or when by Music, the most entrancing of the Poetic moods—we find ourselves melted into tears—not as the Abbaté Gravia supposes—through excess of pleasure, but through a certain petulant, impatient sorrow at our inability to grasp *now* wholly, here on earth, at once and forever, those divine and rapturous joys, of which *through* the poem, or *through* the music, we attain to but brief and indeterminate glimpses.

The struggle to apprehend the supernal Loveliness—this struggle, on the part of souls fittingly constituted—has given to the world all *that* which it (the world) has ever been enabled at once to understand and *to feel* as poetic.

The Poetic Sentiment, of course, may develop itself in various modes—in Painting, in Sculpture, in Architecture, in the Dance—very especially in Music,—and very peculiarly, and with a wide field, in the composition of the Landscape Garden. Our present theme, however, has regard only to its manifestation in words. And here let me speak briefly on the topic of rhythm. Contenting myself with the certainty that Music, in its various modes of metre, rhythm, and rhyme, is of so vast a moment in Poetry as never to be wisely rejected—is so vitally important an adjunct, that he is simply silly who declines its assistance, I will not now pause to maintain its absolute essentiality. It is in Music, perhaps, that the soul most nearly attains the great end for which, when inspired by the Poetic Sentiment, it struggles—the creation of supernal Beauty. It *may* be, indeed, that here this sublime end is, now and then, attained *in fact*. We are often made to feel, with a shivering delight, that from an earthly harp are stricken notes which *cannot* have been unfamiliar to the angels. And thus there can be little doubt that in the union of Poetry with Music in its popular sense, we shall find the widest field for the Poetic development. The old Bards and Minnesingers had advantages which we do not possess—and Thomas Moore, singing his own songs, was, in the most legitimate manner, perfecting them as poems.

To recapitulate, then:—I would define, in brief, the Poetry of words as *The Rhythmical Creation of Beauty.* Its sole arbiter is Taste. With the Intellect or with the Conscience, it has only collateral relations. Unless incidentally, it has no concern whatever either with Duty or with Truth.

A few words, however, in explanation. *That* pleasure which is at once the most pure, the most elevating, and the most intense, is derived, I maintain, from the contemplation of the Beautiful. In the contemplation of Beauty we alone find it possible to attain that pleasurable elevation, or excitement, *of the soul,* which we recognize as the Poetic Sentiment, and which is so easily distinguished from Truth, which is the satisfaction of the Reason, or from Passion, which is the excitement of the Heart. I make Beauty, therefore,—using the word as inclusive of the sublime,—I make Beauty the province of the poem, simply because it is an obvious rule of Art that effects should be made to spring as directly as possible from their causes—no one as yet having been weak enough to deny that the peculiar elevation in question is at least *most readily* attainable in the poem. It by no means follows, however, that the incitements of Passion, or the precepts of Duty, or even the lessons of Truth, may not be introduced into a poem, and with advantage; for they may subserve, incidentally, in various ways, the general purposes of the work; but the true artist will always contrive to tone them down in proper subjection to that *Beauty* which is the atmosphere and the real essence of the poem.

I cannot better introduce the few poems which I shall present for your consideration, than by the citation of the Proem to Mr. Longfellow's "Waif":

> The day is done, and the darkness
>   Falls from the wings of Night,
> As a feather is wafted downward
>   From an Eagle in his flight.
>
> I see the lights of the village
>   Gleam through the rain and the mist,
> And a feeling of sadness comes o'er me,
>   That my soul cannot resist;
>
> A feeling of sadness and longing,
>   That is not akin to pain,
> And resembles sorrow only
>   As the mist resembles the rain.
>
> Come, read to me some poem,
>   Some simple and heartfelt lay,
> That shall soothe this restless feeling
>   And banish the thoughts of day.
>
> Not from the grand old masters,
>   Not from the bards sublime,
> Whose distant footsteps echo
>   Through the corridors of time.
>
> For, like strains of martial music,
>   Their mighty thoughts suggest
> Life's endless toil and endeavor;
>   And to-night I long for rest.
>
> Read from some humbler poet,
>   Whose songs gushed from his heart,

As showers from the clouds of summer,
    Or tears from the eyelids start;

Who through long days of labor,
    And nights devoid of ease,
Still heard in his soul the music
    Of wonderful melodies.

Such songs have power to quiet
    The restless pulse of care,
And come like the benediction
    That follows after prayer.

Then read from the treasured volume
    The poem of thy choice,
And lend to the rhyme of the poet
    The beauty of thy voice.

And the night shall be filled with music,
    And the cares, that infest the day,
Shall fold their tents, like the Arabs,
    And as silently steal away.

With no great range of imagination, these lines have been justly admired for their delicacy of expression. Some of the images are very effective. Nothing can be better than—

    ——the bards sublime,
Whose distant footsteps echo
    Through the corridors of time.

The idea of the last quatrain is also very effective. The poem, on the whole, however, is chiefly to be admired for the graceful *insouciance* of its metre, so well in accordance with the character of the sentiments, and especially for the *ease* of the general manner. This "ease," or naturalness, in a literary style, it has long been the fashion to regard as ease in appearance alone—as a point of really difficult attainment. But not so,—a natural manner is difficult only to him who should never meddle with it—to the unnatural. It is but the result of writing with the understanding, or with the instinct, that *the tone,* in composition, should always be that which the mass of mankind would adopt—and must perpetually vary, of course, with the occasion. The author who, after the fashion of the *North American Review,* should be, upon *all* occasions, merely "quiet," must necessarily, upon *many* occasions, be simply silly, or stupid; and has no more right to be considered, "easy," or "natural," than a Cockney exquisite, or than the sleeping Beauty in the wax-works.

Among the minor poems of Bryant, none has so much impressed me as the one which he entitles "June." I quote only a portion of it:

> There, through the long, long summer hours,
>   The golden light should lie,
> And thick, young herbs and groups of flowers
>   Stand in their beauty by.
> The oriole should build and tell
> His love-tale, close beside my cell;
>   The idle butterfly
> Should rest him there, and there be heard
> The housewife-bee and humming-bird.
>
> And what, if cheerful shouts, at noon,
>   Come, from the village sent,
> Or songs of maids, beneath the moon,
>   With fairy laughter blent?
> And what if, in the evening light,
> Betrothèd lovers walk in sight
>   Of my low monument?

I would the lovely scene around
Might know no sadder sight nor sound.

I know, I know I should not see
    The season's glorious show,
Nor would its brightness shine for me,
    Nor its wild music flow;
But if, around my place of sleep,
The friends I love should come to weep,
    They might not haste to go.
Soft airs, and song, and light, and bloom
Should keep them, lingering by my tomb.

These to their soften'd hearts should bear
    The thought of what has been,
And speak of one who cannot share
    The gladness of the scene;
Whose part in all the pomp that fills
The circuit of the summer hills,
    Is—that his grave is green;
And deeply would their hearts rejoice
To hear again his living voice.

The rhythmical flow, here, is even voluptuous—nothing could be more melodious. The poem has always affected me in a remarkable manner. The intense melancholy which seems to well up, perforce, to the surface of all the poet's cheerful sayings about his grave, we find thrilling us to the soul—while there is the truest poetic elevation in the thrill. The impression left is one of a pleasurable sadness. And if, in the remaining compositions which I shall introduce to you, there be more or less of a similar tone always apparent, let me remind you that (how or why we know not) this certain taint of sadness is inseparably connected with all the higher manifestations of true Beauty. It is, nevertheless,

A feeling of sadness and longing,
    That is not akin to pain,
And resembles sorrow only
    As the mist resembles the rain.

The taint of which I speak is clearly perceptible even in a poem so full of brilliancy and spirit as the "Health" of Edward C. Pinkney:

I fill this cup to one made up
    Of loveliness alone,
A woman, of her gentle sex
    The seeming paragon;
To whom the better elements
    And kindly stars have given
A form so fair, that, like the air,
    'Tis less of earth than heaven.

Her every tone is music's own,
    Like those of morning birds,
And something more than melody
    Dwells ever in her words:
The coinage of her heart are they,
    And from her lips each flows
As one may see the burden'd bee
    Forth issue from the rose.

Affections are as thoughts to her,
    The measures of her hours;
Her feelings have the fragrancy,
    The freshness of young flowers;
And lovely passions, changing oft,
    So fill her, she appears
The image of themselves by turns,—
    The idol of past years!

Of her bright face one glance will trace
　　A picture on the brain,
And of her voice in echoing hearts
　　A sound must long remain;
But memory, such as mine of her,
　　So very much endears,
When death is nigh my latest sigh
　　Will not be life's, but hers.

I fill'd this cup to one made up
　　Of loveliness alone,
A woman, of her gentle sex
　　The seeming paragon—
Her health! and would on earth there stood
　　Some more of such a frame,
That life might be all poetry,
　　And weariness a name.

It was the misfortune of Mr. Pinkney to have been born too far south. Had
he been a New Englander, it is probable that he would have been ranked as
the first of American lyrists, by that magnanimous cabal which has so long
controlled the destinies of American Letters, in conducting the thing called
the *North American Review.* The poem just cited is especially beautiful; but
the poetic elevation which it induces, we must refer chiefly to our sympathy
in the poet's enthusiasm. We pardon his hyperboles for the evident
earnestness with which they are uttered.

It is by no means my design, however, to expatiate upon the *merits* of what
I should read you. These will necessarily speak for themselves. Boccalini, in
his "Advertisements from Parnassus," tells us that Zoilus once presented
Apollo a very caustic criticism upon a very admirable book—whereupon
the god asked him for the beauties of the work. He replied that he only

busied himself about the errors. On hearing this, Apollo, handing him a sack of unwinnowed wheat, bade him pick out *all the chaff* for his reward.

Now this fable answers very well as a hit at the critics—but I am by no means sure that the god was in the right. I am by no means certain that the true limits of the critical duty are not grossly misunderstood. Excellence, in a poem especially, may be considered in the light of an axiom, which need only be properly *put* to become self-evident. It is *not* excellence if it requires to be demonstrated as such:—and thus, to point out too particularly the merits of a work of Art, is to admit that they are *not* merits altogether.

Among the "Melodies" of Thomas Moore, is one whose distinguished character as a poem proper seems to have been singularly left out of view. I allude to his lines beginning: "Come, rest in this bosom." The intense energy of their expression is not surpassed by any thing in Byron. There are two of the lines in which a sentiment is conveyed that embodies the *all in all* of the divine passion of Love—a sentiment which, perhaps, has found its echo in more, and in more passionate, human hearts than any other single sentiment ever embodied in words:

> Come, rest in this bosom, my own stricken deer,
> Though the herd have fled from thee, thy home is still here;
> Here still is the smile that no cloud can o'ercast,
> And a heart and a hand all thy own to the last.
>
> Oh! what was love made for, if 'tis not the same
> Through joy and through torment, through glory and shame?
> I know not, I ask not, if guilt's in that heart,
> I but know that I love thee, whatever thou art.
>
> Thou hast call'd me thy Angel in moments of bliss.
> And thy Angel I'll be, 'mid the horrors of this,—
> Through the furnace, unshrinking, thy steps to pursue,
> And shield thee, and save thee,—or perish there too!

It has been the fashion, of late days, to deny Moore Imagination, while granting him Fancy—a distinction originating with Coleridge—than whom no man more fully comprehended the great powers of Moore. The fact is, that the fancy of this poet so far predominates over all his other faculties, and over the fancy of all other men, as to have induced, very naturally, the idea that he is fanciful *only.* But never was there a greater mistake. Never was a grosser wrong done the fame of a true poet. In the compass of the English language I can call to mind no poem more profoundly, more weirdly *imaginative,* in the best sense, than the lines commencing: "I would I were by that dim lake," which are the composition of Thomas Moore. I regret that I am unable to remember them.

One of the noblest—and, speaking of Fancy, one of the most singularly fanciful—of modern poets, was Thomas Hood. His "Fair Ines" had always, for me, an inexpressible charm:

> Oh! saw ye not fair Ines?
>   She's gone into the West,
> To dazzle when the sun is down,
>   And rob the world of rest:
> She took our daylight with her,
>   The smiles that we love best,
> With morning blushes on her cheek,
>   And pearls upon her breast.
>
> Oh! turn again, fair Ines,
>   Before the fall of night,
> For fear the moon should shine alone,
>   And stars unrivall'd bright;
> And blessèd will the lover be
>   That walks beneath their light,

And breathes the love against thy cheek
    I dare not even write!

Would I had been, fair Ines,
    That gallant cavalier,
Who rode so gayly by thy side,
    And whisper'd thee so near!

Were there no bonny dames at home,
    Or no true lovers here,
That he should cross the seas to win
    The dearest of the dear?

I saw thee, lovely Ines,
    Descend along the shore,
With bands of noble gentlemen,
    And banners waved before;
And gentle youth and maidens gay,
    And snowy plumes they wore;
It would have been a beauteous dream,
    —If it had been no more!

Alas, alas, fair Ines!
    She went away with song,
With Music waiting on her steps,
    And shoutings of the throng;
But some were sad and felt no mirth,
    But only Music's wrong,
In sounds that sang Farewell, Farewell,
    To her you've loved so long.

Farewell, farewell, fair Ines,
    That vessel never bore
So fair a lady on its deck,
    Nor danced so light before.

Alas for pleasure on the sea,
    And sorrow on the shore!
The smile that blessed one lover's heart
    Has broken many more.

"The Haunted House," by the same author, is one of the truest poems ever written—one of the *truest*—one of the most unexceptionable—one of the most thoroughly artistic, both in its theme and in its execution. It is, moreover, powerfully ideal—imaginative. I regret that its length renders it unsuitable for the purposes of this Lecture. In place of it, permit me to offer the universally appreciated "Bridge of Sighs."

One more unfortunate,
Weary of breath,
Rashly importunate,
Gone to her death!

Take her up tenderly,
Lift her with care;
Fashion'd so slenderly,
Young, and so fair!

Look at her garments
Clinging like cerements;
Whilst the wave constantly
Drips from her clothing;
Take her up instantly,
Loving, not loathing.—

Touch her not scornfully;
Think of her mournfully,
Gently and humanly;
Not of the stains of her,
All that remains of her
Now, is pure womanly.

Make no deep scrutiny
Into her mutiny
Rash and undutiful:
Past all dishonor,
Death has left on her
Only the beautiful.

Still, for all slips of hers
One of Eve's family—
Wipe those poor lips of hers
Oozing so clammily.

Loop up her tresses
Escaped from the comb,
Her fair auburn tresses;
Whilst wonderment guesses
Where was her home?

Who was her father?
Who was her mother?
Had she a sister?
Had she a brother?
Or was there a dearer one
Still, and a nearer one
Yet, than all other?

Alas! for the rarity
Of Christian charity
Under the sun!
Oh, it was pitiful!
Near a whole city full,
Home she had none.

Sisterly, brotherly,
Fatherly, motherly

Feelings had changed:
Love, by harsh evidence
Thrown from its eminence;
Even God's providence
Seeming estranged.

Where the lamps quiver
So far in the river,
With many a light
From window and casement,
From garret to basement,
She stood, with amazement,
Houseless by night.

The bleak wind of March
Made her tremble and shiver;
But not the dark arch,
Or the black flowing river:
Mad from life's history,
Glad to death's mystery,
Swift to be hurl'd—
Anywhere, anywhere
Out of the world!

In she plunged boldly,
No matter how coldly
The rough river ran,—
Over the brink of it,
Picture it—think of it,
Dissolute man!
Lave in it, drink of it
Then, if you can!

Take her up tenderly,
Lift her with care;
Fashion'd so slenderly,
Young, and so fair!

Ere her limbs frigidly
Stiffen too rigidly,
Decently,—kindly,—
Smooth, and compose them;
And her eyes, close them,
Staring so blindly!

Dreadfully staring
Through muddy impurity,
As when with the daring
Last look of despairing
Fixed on futurity.

Perishing gloomily,
Spurred by contumely,
Cold inhumanity,
Burning insanity,
Into her rest.—
Cross her hands humbly,
As if praying dumbly,
Over her breast!

Owning her weakness,
Her evil behavior,
And leaving, with meekness,
Her sins to her Saviour!

The vigor of this poem is no less remarkable than its pathos. The
versification, although carrying the fanciful to the very verge of the

fantastic, is nevertheless admirably adapted to the wild insanity which is the thesis of the poem.

Among the minor poems of Lord Byron, is one which has never received from the critics the praise which it undoubtedly deserves:

> Though the day of my destiny's over,
>   And the star of my fate hath declined,
> Thy soft heart refused to discover
>   The faults which so many could find;
> Though thy soul with my grief was acquainted
>   It shrunk not to share it with me,
> And the love which my spirit hath painted
>   It never hath found but in *thee*.
>
> Then when nature around me is smiling,
>   The last smile which answers to mine,
> I do not believe it beguiling,
>   Because it reminds me of thine;
> And when winds are at war with the ocean,
>   As the breasts I believed in with me,
> If their billows excite an emotion,
>   It is that they bear me from *thee*.
>
> Though the rock of my last hope is shivered,
>   And its fragments are sunk in the wave,
> Though I feel that my soul is delivered
>   To pain—it shall not be its slave.
> There is many a pang to pursue me;
>   They may crush, but they shall not contemn;
> They may torture, but shall not subdue me;
>   'Tis of *thee* that I think—not of them.
>
> Though human, thou didst not deceive me;
>   Though woman, thou didst not forsake;

Though loved, thou forborest to grieve me;
   Though slandered, thou never couldst shake;
Though trusted, thou didst not disclaim me;
   Though parted, it was not to fly;
Though watchful, 'twas not to defame me;
   Nor mute, that the world might belie.

Yet I blame not the world, nor despise it,
   Nor the war of the many with one—
If my soul was not fitted to prize it,
   'Twas folly not sooner to shun:
And if dearly that error hath cost me,
   And more than I once could foresee,
I have found that whatever it lost me,
   It could not deprive me of *thee*.

From the wreck of the past, which hath perished,
   Thus much I at least may recall:
It hath taught me that which I most cherished
   Deserved to be dearest of all.
In the desert a fountain is springing,
   In the wide waste there still is a tree,
And a bird in the solitude singing,
   Which speaks to my spirit of *thee*.

Although the rhythm here is one of the most difficult, the versification could scarcely be improved. No nobler *theme* ever engaged the pen of poet. It is the soul-elevating idea, that no man can consider himself entitled to complain of Fate while, in his adversity, he still retains the unwavering love of woman.

From Alfred Tennyson—although in perfect sincerity I regard him as the noblest poet that ever lived—I have left myself time to cite only a very brief specimen. I call him, and *think* him the noblest of poets—*not* because the impressions he produces are, at all times, the most profound—*not* because the poetical excitement which he induces is, at *all* times, the most intense—but because it *is,* at all times, the most ethereal—in other words, the most elevating and the most pure. No poet is so little of the earth, earthy. What I am about to read is from his last long poem, "The Princess":

> Tears, idle tears, I know not what they mean,
> Tears from the depth of some divine despair
> Rise in the heart, and gather to the eyes,
> In looking on the happy autumn-fields,
> And thinking of the days that are no more.
>
> Fresh as the first beam glittering on a sail
> That brings our friends up from the underworld,
> Sad as the last which reddens over one
> That sinks with all we love below the verge;
> So sad, so fresh, the days that are no more.
>
> Ah, sad and strange as in dark summer dawns
> The earliest pipe of half-awaken'd birds
> To dying ears, when unto dying eyes
> The casement slowly grows a glimmering square;
> So sad, so strange, the days that are no more.
>
> Dear as remember'd kisses after death,
> And sweet as those by hopeless fancy feign'd
> On lips that are for others; deep as love,
> Deep as first love, and wild with all regret;
> O Death in Life, the days that are no more!

Thus, although in a very cursory and imperfect manner, I have endeavored to convey to you my conception of the Poetic Principle. It has been my purpose to suggest that, while this Principle itself is, strictly and simply, the Human Aspiration for Supernal Beauty, the manifestation of the Principle is always found in *an elevating excitement of the Soul*—quite independent of that passion which is the intoxication of the Heart—or of that Truth which is the satisfaction of the Reason. For, in regard to Passion, alas! its tendency is to degrade rather than elevate the Soul. Love, on the contrary—Love—the true, the divine Eros—the Uranian, as distinguished from the Dionaean Venus—is unquestionably the purest and truest of all poetical themes. And in regard to Truth—if, to be sure, through the attainment of a truth, we are led to perceive a harmony where none was apparent before, we experience, at once, the true poetical effect—but this effect is referable to the harmony alone, and not in the least degree to the truth which merely served to render the harmony manifest.

We shall reach, however, more immediately a distinct conception of what the true Poetry is, by mere reference to a few of the simple elements which induce in the Poet himself the true poetical effect. He recognizes the ambrosia which nourishes his soul, in the bright orbs that shine in Heaven—in the volutes of the flower—in the clustering of low shrubberies—in the waving of the grain-fields—in the slanting of the tall, Eastern trees—in the blue distance of mountains—in the grouping of clouds—in the twinkling of half-hidden brooks—in the gleaming of silver rivers—in the repose of sequestered lakes—in the star-mirroring depths of lonely wells. He perceives it in the songs of birds—in the harp of Æolus—in the sighing of the night-wind—in the repining voice of the forest—in the surf that complains to the shore—in the fresh breath of the woods—in the scent of the violet—in the voluptuous perfume of the hyacinth—in the suggestive odor that comes to him, at eventide, from far-distant, undiscovered islands, over dim oceans, illimitable and unexplored. He owns it in all noble thoughts—in all unworldly motives—in all holy impulses—in all chivalrous, generous, and self-sacrificing deeds. He feels it in the beauty of woman—in the grace of her step—in the lustre of her eye—in the melody of her voice—in her soft laughter—in her sigh—in the harmony of the rustling of her robes. He deeply feels it in her winning endearments—in her burning enthusiasms—in her gentle charities—in her meek and devotional endurances—but above all—ah! far above all—he kneels to it—he worships it in the faith, in the purity, in the strength, in the altogether divine majesty—of her *love*.

Let me conclude by the recitation of yet another brief poem—one very different in character from any that I have before quoted. It is by Mother-well, and is called "The Song of the Cavalier." With our modern and altogether rational ideas of the absurdity and impiety of warfare, we are not precisely in that frame of mind best adapted to sympathize with the sentiments, and thus to appreciate the real excellence, of the poem. To do this fully, we must identify ourselves, in fancy, with the soul of the old cavalier.

> Then mounte! then mounte, brave gallants, all,
>   And don your helmes amaine:
> Deathe's couriers, Fame and Honor, call
>   Us to the field againe.
>
> No shrewish teares shall fill our eye
>   When the sword-hilt's in our hand,—
> Heart-whole we'll part and no whit sighe
>   For the fayrest of the land;
> Let piping swaine, and craven wight,
>   Thus weepe and puling crye,
> Our business is like men to fight,
>   And hero-like to die!